A DICTIONARY OF
MAORI PLACE NAMES

A DICTIONARY OF
MAORI PLACE NAMES

By A. W. REED

Illustrated by James Berry

REED

Published by Reed Books,
a division of Reed Publishing (NZ) Ltd,
39 Rawene Road, Birkenhead, Auckland. Associated
companies, branches and representatives throughout
the world.

ISBN 0 7900 0040 7

First published 1961
Reprinted 1963, 1969, 1972, 1974, 1978
Second edition 1982
Reprinted 1983, 1985, 1986, 1987, 1988, 1990, 1991, 1992, 1994

Printed by Kings Time Printing Press Ltd, Hong Kong

FOREWORD

THIS book is the successor to *Maori Place Names and their Meanings,* which was first published in 1950 and which has been reprinted a number of times. It is now felt that the time has come when it should be completely revised, and enlarged by the inclusion of more factual material than the earlier book was able to provide.

A personal word of explanation may not be out of place. *Maori Place Names and their Meanings* was compiled by the present author because of the need that had been expressed for a book of this kind. Information was sought from obvious sources such as the *New Zealand Official Year Book* for 1919, in which the late Elsdon Best had given a brief list of meanings of Maori names; Mr. Johannes C. Andersen's *Maori Place Names;* Mr. G. G. M. Mitchell's *Maori Place Names of Buller County,* and other works which were readily accessible.

It was realised at the time that there are many problems to be faced in attempting a literal translation of Maori place names, many of which go back to early days; some indeed were used in the homeland of Hawaiki and transplanted to the soil of Aotearoa (New Zealand). Others had their origins in history and legend and have been lost, or are too long to recount in a small book. Some names have suffered alteration and distortion; some are modern names; some are too easily translated, giving false and ludicrous conclusions; and some are quite untranslatable.

On the other hand the Maori was closer to nature than the Pakeha (white man); common words for wood and water, wind and cloud and soil were frequently incorporated in his names. Commonsense and direct translation provided most of the answers in the original collection, although it was always acknowledged that a more comprehensive and documented work would eventually be required.

As it happened, the task of putting together the first reference

5

book was the start of a fascinating hobby, which has resulted in a collection of the origins of place names in New Zealand. The fruits of some of this work will be found in the present book.

The information contained in *Maori Place Names* has been gathered from hundreds of books, and through correspondence and conversation with many who are able to provide specialised knowledge in different parts of the country.

Some of the limitations of the first collection still apply, for a really satisfactory answer can seldom be supplied to the question "What does this name mean?" The Pakeha reader will realise how futile it would be to attempt to translate English names in New Zealand for the benefit of Maori readers; what would he make, for instance, of such names as Gore, Nightcaps, Huntly, Cashmere, Fortrose, Dunedin, Auckland, Shotover and Drury? A similar problem faces us when we attempt to make a literal translation of Maori names.

On the other hand, sufficient historical and legendary tradition has been preserved to enable us to say with some certainty how some names were determined, and to give their meanings. We trust that the interested reader may find interesting glimpses of Maori life in the short notes which are attached to some of the names.

In order to assist the reader, the names have been broken up into their several components, with a translation of the words which these comprise. If sense can be made of the resulting words, a meaning has been attempted. But it must be emphasised that this meaning is no more than an attempt at translating a word, a phrase or a sentence from one language to another. The interested reader who is equipped with a Maori dictionary may himself arrive at an equally satisfying translation.

A comprehensive selection of names has been made, but a large volume would be required to include every Maori place. All the best-known and more important Maori names are included, but there is also a selection of older names which are no longer in use but which most readers may come across at some time or another—an obvious example is Aorangi, the Maori name for Mount Cook. Some lesser-known names are mentioned because of the interest attached to their origin.

The appendix consists of Pakeha names to which reference is made in the text. These may be Pakeha names which have replaced the original Maori name, or they may list Maori place-names in towns and cities; e.g., under Wellington will be found references to the suburbs of Hataitai and Rongotai, which are listed in the main part of the book.

Some thought has been spent on the question of giving an indication of the location of the various places, but it is felt that this is outside the scope of the present book. Such a gazetteer would suffer through the absence of Pakeha names and by the frequent duplication of Maori names, e.g., Wairoa found again and again in various parts of New Zealand.

It is hoped that this excursion into the meanings of Maori place names will prove stimulating to the reader, who may well be encouraged to make his own investigations. To assist those who are interested, or who may require the meaning of a name of some place not included in this book, a list of words which commonly form a part of Maori place names will be found at the beginning of the book. Readers who wish to extend their interest in the subject are recommended to *Reeds' Concise Maori Dictionary;* those whose studies carry them further would be well advised to seek Williams's *Dictionary of the Maori Language.*

A. W. REED

HINTS ON PRONUNCIATION

There are only fifteen letters in the Maori alphabet :

A E H I K M N O P R T U W NG and WH.

Every syllable in Maori ends in a vowel, which makes the proportion of vowels to consonants much higher than in English. The vowel sounds are therefore of great importance. While the quantity of each of these vowels may vary, and thus change the meaning of a word, such differences are beyond the capacity of the average Pakeha. The following list should be learned by heart :

A is always pronounced as the a in "rather".
E is always pronounced as the e in "ten".
I is always pronounced like the ee in "seen".
O is always pronounced like the o in "border".
U is always pronounced like the oo in "bloom".

When two vowels come together each is given its proper sound.

The compound consonants NG and WH. These are the two stumbling blocks in the way of correct pronunciation. The sound NG is that of the middle NG in the word "singing".

WH is usually pronounced as F. This is not the correct sound, which has been described as F, but without letting the top teeth touch the lower lip. If you cannot manage this, the sound of F will pass muster.

These are simple rules, but if they are mastered you will never again be guilty of referring to TE AWAMUTU as TEE-AMOOT, or to WANGANUI as WANGGANUEE.

WORDS WHICH COMMONLY FORM PART OF MAORI PLACE NAMES

AHI : fire.

AO : cloud.

ARA : path or road.

ATA : shadow.

ATUA : god.

AWA : river, channel, gully or valley.

HAKA : dance.

HAU : wind.

HUA : fruit, egg.

IKA : fish.

ITI : small.

KAI : food, or eat.

KINO : bad.

MA : white or clear.

MA : (short for *manga*) : branch or tributary or stream.

MANGA : branch, tributary or stream.

MANU : bird.

MATA : headland, and many other meanings.

MAUNGA : mountain.

MOANA : sea.

MOTU : island.

MURI : end.

MUTU : end, finished.

NUI : big, or plenty of.

O : of, or the place of.

ONE : mud, sand or beach.

PA : fortified village.

PAE : ridge, or resting place.

PAPA : broad, flat, or ground covered with vegetation.

PO : night.

PUKE : hill.

PUNA : spring of water.

RANGI : sky.

RAU : hundred, many or leaf.

RIKI : small or few.

ROA : long or high.

ROTO : lake.

RUA : cave, hollow or two.

TAHI : one, single.

TAI : sea, coast or tide.

TAPU : forbidden or sacred.

TEA : white, or clear.

WAI : water.

WAKA : canoe.

WHANGA : bay, inlet, or stretch of water.

WHARE : house.

WHATA : raised platform for storing food.

WHENUA : land or country.

MAORI PLACE NAMES

AHAURA : Probably a corrupt form of O-hauroa. *o:* the place of; *hauroa:* height. As the township of Ahaura is on an elevation, and the local Maoris say that the name means a cliff, the meaning is doubtless The place of a cliff.

AHIARUHE : *ahi:* fire; *aruhe:* fern-root. Fire for roasting fern-root. Fern-root was an important food for the Maori. It was roasted before a fire and pounded with wooden beaters.

AHIKIWI : *ahi:* fire; *kiwi:* flightless bird. Fire on which kiwis were cooked.

AHIMANAWA : *ahi·* fire; *manawa:* heart. A chief named Tarewa-a-rua was slain by his enemies. His heart was torn out, cooked, and eaten. The Ahimanawa Range has a similar origin. To avenge himself for the death of his daughter, the chief Te Kohipipi surprised his enemies by night. In the early morning he cut out the hearts of those he had killed. He put them in a flax kit and took them home. Half-way up

the range he rested, lit a fire and ate some of the hearts. The range was then known as Te Ahi-manawa-a-Te-Kohipipi (The fire of the hearts of Te Kohipipi).

AHIPARA : *ahi:* fire; *para:* various roots used for food. Fire for roasting fern-root.

AHITARAKIHI : *ahi:* fire; *tarakihi:* an edible fish. Fire at which the tarakihi was roasted.

AHITITI : *ahi:* fire; *titi:* mutton-bird. Fire for cooking mutton-birds.

AHUAHU : to heap up. This is the Maori name for Great Mercury Island. Paikea came to this island on the back of a whale. He was cold and heaped the warm sand over him, and from this circumstance he gave the island its name.

AHURIRI : Named after Tu Ahuriri who found the lagoon blocked so that the flood destroyed the shellfish. He organised a working party to clear a channel to the sea, and the area was named after him. The missionary Colenso, however, said that the name means "fierce rushing", which was an allusion to the swift current in the channel where the river runs into the sea.

AHUROA : *ahu:* heap or mound; *roa:* long.

AKAAKA : Fibrous roots.

AKARANA : The Maori form of Auckland.

AKAROA : *aka* (South Island form of *whanga*): harbour; *roa:* long. Long harbour.

AKATARAWA : The original form of the name may have been Akatarewa. *aka:* vine; *tarewa:* trailing. Trailing vines.

AKATORE : The correct spelling is Akatorea. *Aka* is the South Island form of *whanga:* harbour; *torea:* wading bird. Torea harbour.

AKEAKE : a native tree.

AKERAMA : This is the Maori form of the name Aceldama, "field of blood", the name being given at the time that the first missionaries came to North Auckland.

AKITIO : *aki:* to smash; *tio:* piercing cold. It is said that the name came from a famous greenstone mere (club).

AMOKURA : The name of tropical bird which visits New Zealand. It is distinguished by two brilliant red tail feathers. The name was given in 1929.

AMURI : Correctly the name should be Haumuri, which means an east wind, or "the wind at your back".

ANAKIWA : *ana:* cave; *a:* of; *Kiwa:* a man's name. Kiwa was also one of the gods of the ocean. The cave of Kiwa.

ANATOKI : *ana:* cave; *toki:* adze. Cave of the adze.

ANAURA : This may be a name which has come from Mangaia in the Cook Islands. In a true Maori form it would be Anakura. *ana:* cave; *kura:* red. Red cave.

ANAWHAKAIRO : *ana:* cave; *whakairo:* to paint or carve in a pattern. In this cave on the banks of the Waitaki

Toki: adze

River near Coal Creek, the water has carved out recesses in the rock wall, and there are fantastically shaped pinnacles, and round window-like holes. Cave of carved or sculptured rock.

ANAWHATA: *ana:* cave; *whata:* food store. Cave of the food store.

ANIWANIWA: Rainbow.

AOHANGA: A variety of flax. The name has appeared at various times as Ohonga, Ohanga, and Aohanga, but the proper form is probably Owahanga. *o:* the place of; *wahanga:* mouths. The name was applied to the river as a whole.

AOKAPARANGI: *ao:* cloud; *kapa:* row or rank; *rangi:* sky. A row of clouds in the sky.

AOKAUTERE: *ao:* cloud; *kautere:* to float or move swiftly. Swiftly moving clouds.

AONGATETE: *ao:* cloud; *ngatete:* to move. Moving clouds.

AORANGI: *ao:* cloud; *rangi:* sky. Cloud in the sky. This is one of the best-known names in New Zealand, because it is the Maori name for Mount Cook, the highest mountain peak in the country. It is popularly translated Skypiercer, but this is not the real meaning of the name. The South Island Maoris called it Aoraki, because *raki* is the S.I. pronunciation of *rangi*. There are several versions of the true origin of the name. It is said to be named after well-known peaks in the Cook and Society groups of islands at which the Maoris called on their way to New Zealand.

Then there is a romantic legend connected with the arrival of the famous Arai-te-uru canoe which came from Hawaiki in the fourteenth century. The canoe was wrecked and the crew travelled by land northwards through the Mackenzie country. When they sighted Mount Cook they noticed that it was higher than any of the other peaks which had been named after members of the party. They looked round them to see who was the tallest in order that his name might be given to the mountain, and it was found that the one who was tallest was a little boy named Aorangi who was being carried on the shoulders of his grandfather.

There is another story which goes even further back into time, when the gods were to be found on the earth. Some of the sky children came to earth in a canoe which was called Te Waka-a-Aorangi (the canoe of Aorangi). The canoe was turned to stone and became the South Island. Aorangi, the captain of the canoe, was turned into the mountain we know as Mount Cook. He had three brothers, Rangi-roa, Rangi-rua, and Rarangi-roa. They were turned into mountains too and became Mounts Dampier, Teichelmann, and the Silberhorn.

The name is applied to many other parts of New Zealand and sometimes it has an entirely different origin. There is a place of this name near Feilding. Here called the famous explorer Tamatea who was on his way to Wanganui. He left a lizard there and called the place Aorangi. It is possible that it was named after the lizard.

The Aorangi Range is misnamed, as it was originally Haurangi. The pronunciation of the two names is very similar.

AORERE: *ao:* cloud or mist; *rere:* flying. Flying scud or mist. Nowadays the Maori calls an aeroplane *ao-rere* or *manu-rere* (flying bird).

AOROA: *ao:* cloud; *roa:* long. Long cloud.

AOTEA: The name of the canoe in which Turi came to New Zealand. The Aotea gave its name to a small harbour on the west coast of the North Island where the immigrants first landed. It was also the Maori name of Great Barrier Island.

There is a farming district in Marlborough which was so named by Archdeacon Grace because it means sunny spot.

AOTEAROA: The usual meaning given to the Maori name for New Zealand is Land of the long white cloud. *ao:* cloud; *tea:* white; *roa:* long. But this is only one of several possible meanings. The following interpretations have been given by various authorities: Long white cloud; Continuously clear light; Big glaring light; Land of abiding day; Long white world; Long bright world; Long daylight; Long lingering day; Long bright land; Long bright day. Most of these meanings can be justified because *ao* means both cloud and day, and *tea* both white and bright.

When Kupe, the first discoverer of New Zealand, first came in sight of the land, his wife cried, "He ao! He ao!" (a cloud! a cloud!). Great Barrier Island was therefore named Aotea (white cloud), and the long mainland Aotearoa (long white cloud). When Kupe finally returned to his homeland his people asked him why he did not call the newly discovered country after his fatherland. He replied, "I preferred the warm breast to the cold one, the new land to the old land long forsaken."

Nevertheless the name still provides some problems which may never be fully solved.

AOTUHIA : *ao:* daylight; *tuhia:* to glow. Glowing daylight.

AOWHENUA : *ao:* daylight; *whenua:* land or country. Land of daylight.

APARIMA : *apa:* a party of workmen; *rima:* five. The name is almost certainly that of a celebrated Waitaha chieftainess of long ago. Another theory is that the name is the Maori form of Apolima, an island in the Pacific known to the Maori before the migration.

There is an interesting but suspect conjecture that the name means "five-fold streams" or "five-fold ridges". From five ridges the Aparima River receives five tributaries, which are known as the Five Rivers district.

APITI : Narrow pass or gorge.

APOKA : This small inlet in Marlborough is named after a Maori, Ihone Apoka, who lived there.

APONGA : Gathered together or heaped up.

ARA-A-KIWA : The path of Kiwa. The Maori name for Foveaux Strait. Kiwa was an ocean god.

ARAHIWI : *ara:* track or path; *hiwi:* ridge or hill-top. A descriptive name. Path over the ridge.

ARAHURA : *ara:* path; *hura:* to discover. The name is connected with Ngahue who was the companion of Kupe on his discovery of New Zealand. Ara'ura is the ancient name of Aitutaki in the Cook Islands, and the landing place and river in the South Island were possibly named in memory of the island home.

On the other hand, it may be that Kupe and Ngahue, after a battle with an octopus in Cook Strait, went down to the west coast of the South Island to search for any people they could find. Ngahue gave the name to perpetuate their search. It was also an early name for the South Island.

ARAI : Screen or veil.

ARAI-TE-URU: The name of the early canoe which was wrecked at Moeraki. Applied originally to Shag Point.

ARAKIHI : *ara:* path; *kihi:* to be cut off.

ARAMATAI : *ara:* path; *matai:* native tree. The path indicated by a matai tree.

ARAMIRO : *ara:* path; *miro:* native tree. This and the previous name may indicate that a path was made across a stream by felling a tree.

ARAMOANA : *ara:* path; *moana:* ocean.

ARAMOHO : The correct form is Aramuhu. *Ara:* path; *muhu:* to force one's way through heavy bush. Over a hundred years ago a Maori named Hau-e-rangi was lost in the dense bush here and wandered about until he died of starvation. When his body was found it was seen that he had beaten an almost circular path in his struggles to find his way out.

ARANGA : The act of rising.

ARANUI : *ara:* path; *nui:* big. There are different origins for different places of this name. In Christchurch it was probably simply descriptive, as the name was only given about the year 1900.

The Aranui Cave at Waitomo was named after a Maori who discovered it while pig-hunting.

The Aranui Creek on the West Coast has an entirely different meaning. *ara:* a small fresh-water fish; *nui:* many. Large numbers of grayling were taken in this creek by the Maoris.

ARAPAEPAE : *ara:* path; *paepae:* ridge. Path along a ridge.

ARAPAOA : *ara:* path; *paoa:* smoke, or blow. The name is an interesting one of importance in Maori tradition, for not only is it the correct form of Arapawa Island, but was once used for the whole of the South Island, and later for the island which Captain Cook landed on to discover Cook Strait. It received its name in one of two ways. It was close to the entrance of Queen Charlotte Sound where Kupe with a downward blow (paoa) killed the enormous octopus Muturangi. The second theory is that early Maoris peered through the mist across the strait which they called "the misty path".

ARAPAWA : *ara:* path; *Pawa:* name of Kupe's slave. Arapawa Island, however, is correctly spelt Arapaoa, q.v.

ARAPITO : *ara:* path; *pito:* end. The Maoris travelled along a well-used track by the Karamea River inland to snare birds and gather berries.

The track ended at a point where the present settlement of Arapito stands.

ARAPOHUE : *ara:* path; *pohue:* convolvulus plant. Path through the convolvulus.

ARAPUNI : *ara:* path; *puni:* blocked, or place of encampment. The meaning may be Path to the camp, a path that has been blocked up by some obstruction.

ARARATA : *ara:* path; *rata:* native tree. Path by or through rata trees.

ARARIMU : *ara:* path; *rimu:* native tree. Path by or through rimu trees.

ARARUA : *ara:* path; *rua:* two. Two paths.

ARATAHA : *ara:* path; *taha:* to pass by.

Rimu: native tree

ARATAPU : *ara:* path; *tapu:* sacred, or prohibited. The sacred path, or Path to a sacred place. The full name is Te Aratapu-o-Manaia. Manaia was a chief who came to New Zealand in the Tokomaru canoe in the 13th or 14th century and landed here on the Wairoa River, Kaipara.

ARATAURA : probably derived from *ara:* path; *tauru:* head or source of a stream. Path by the source of a stream.

ARATIATIA : *ara tiatia:* a series of pegs stuck into the ground to assist in climbing a steep ascent. This descriptive name has been applied to the rapids on the Waikato River because the water seems to zig-zag from one rock to another like the primitive ladders used by the Maori. It may also be connected with the explorer Tia who proceeded up the rapids in his small canoe. It is said that the old river bed was a series of small ledges, each of which carried Tia past another obstacle as he paddled up it.

ARATIKA : *ara:* path; *tika:* straight. Direct path.

ARATORO : *ara:* path; *toro:* to explore, to discover.

ARAWHATA : This may mean a hanging path. A *whata* is a foodstore elevated on a post to keep the contents away from rats. Such stores were sometimes approached by a notched post which was leant against the store, thus providing a series of steps or stairs. Such a stairway was known as an *arawhata,* a path .to the foodstore.

ARERO : Tongue. There is a tradition that there was a battle at this place, and that the victors cut out the tongues of the vanquished.

ARIA : A deep pool, or a stretch of water suitable for fishing by net.

ARIKI-KAPAKAPA: *ariki* is short for *puna-ariki:* hot springs; *kapakapa:* flapping. The name refers to the flapping or fluttering noise made by the hot spring.

AROARO-KAIHE : The Maori name for Mount Sefton. Aroaro-kaihe and her husband Mauka-tu (Ben Ohou) were both members of the crew of the Arai-te-uru canoe.

AROPAOANUI : *aro:* fat covering the kidneys; *paoa nui:* thoroughly bashed. The pa at the mouth of the Aropaoanui river was raided, but the defenders were victorious. In order to celebrate their victory a great feast was prepared with the bodies of the slain. When the ovens were opened up and the cooks were watching the bodies, something happened which caused them to run away in fright and horror. They had seen the bodies moving. They told their chief, Rakai, what they had seen, and he realised at once that it was the kidney fat which was twitching. He went to the ovens and *paoa nui* (thoroughly bashed) the offending portions. From this incident the place received its name.

ARORANGI : *aro:* front; *rangi:* heaven. The front of heaven. The name was brought from the island of Tahiti.

AROWHENUA : *aro:* face or front; *whenua:* land. Several interpretations have been made from time to time, including Good or desirable land; Turning up land for cultivation; and To face or desire land. It is an ancient Polynesian name transplanted to New Zealand.

ATAAHUA : Good, beautiful, or pleasant.

ATAPO : *ata* shadow; *po:* night. Night Shadows.

ATARAU : Moon, or moonlight.

ATAWHAI : Liberality, or kindness.

ATEA : Space. A synonym for Watea, the personified form of space.

ATENE : The Maori form of Athens. The name was given

to the mission station on the Wanganui River by the Rev. Richard Taylor, the original Maori name being O-a-whiti.

ATIAMURI: It was at the Atiamuri Rapids that Tia, the elder brother of the commander of the Arawa canoe, turned back. The name therefore can be broken up into the words A-Tia-muri, *muri* here meaning "turned back".

It has also been conjectured that the word is a contraction of the tribal name Ngati-a-Muri.

ATIU: One of the oldest names in Marlborough, it has probably been transferred from the Cook Islands.

AURIPO: Both *au* and *ripo* mean whirlpool or swirling current.

AUROA: *au:* cloud, mist, or current; *roa:* long.

AWAAWAROA: *awaawa:* valley; *roa:* long. Long valley.

AWAHONU: *awa:* river; *honu:* deep. Deep river.

AWAHOU: *awa:* river; *hou:* new. New river. The Awahou River which flows into Lake Rotorua was named by the explorer Ihenga.

AWAHURI: *awa:* river; *huri:* fascine to turn fish into a river. River with a weir in it.

AWAITI: *awa:* stream; *iti:* small. The place of this name

in Awarua Bay, Nelson, once provided a problem when a Post Office was opened. It could not be called Awarua, its proper name, because there was another Post Office of that name. There were two rivers in the bay, the larger being called Awanui (big river). It was then decided to call the other Awaiti (little river).

AWAKAPONGA: *awa:* stream; *kaponga:* tree-fern. Tree-fern stream.

AWAKARI: *awa:* river; *kari:* isolated clump of trees. River with isolated patches of bush on the banks.

AWAKERI: Ditch.

AWAKINO: *awa:* river; *kino:* bad. Bad river. The Awakino River is still muddy in places, which possibly gave rise to the name.

AWAKOKOMUKA: See under Awamoa.

AWAMANGU: *awa:* river; *mangu:* black. Black river.

AWAMARINO: *awa:* river; *marino:* calm. Calm river.

AWAMATE: *awa:* river; *mate:* dead. Dead river, or Former river. At Awamate in Nelson, a branch of the Motueka River used to run through the place which bore the name.

AWAMOA: *awa:* stream; *moa:* large, extinct flightless

bird. Moa stream. The name was given by W. B. D. Mantell about 1852. The original name was Awakokomuka. *Awa:* stream; *kokomuka:* the South Island name for *koromiko,* a native species of veronica. At the mouth of the stream Mantell discovered ancient ovens of the Waitaha tribe containing moa bones. The stones of the ovens were heated by burning kokomuka, which was considered the best fuel for the purpose. Mantell preferred to call the stream by the more euphonious and appropriate name Awamoa.

AWAMOKIHI: *awa:* river; *mokihi:* a craft made of flax sticks. The stream north of Oamaru was named after a man called Awamokihi.

Moa: extinct giant bird

AWAMOKO: *awa:* stream; *moko:* lizard. Lizard stream.

AWANGA: South-west wind, or a variety of flax or taro.

AWANUI: *awa:* river; *nui:* large, or many. The name may have been brought from Hawaiki.

AWAPUNI: *awa:* river; *puni:* blocked up. It has been suggested that the river may have been blocked up with drift-wood when it was named.

There was a lagoon called Te Awa-puni at Palmerston North, which was an ox-bow or cut off river bend, and could thus be described as a blocked river.

AWAPUTAKITAKI: *awa:* river; *putakitaki:* the South Island form of *putangitangi,* Paradise duck.

AWARERE: *awa:* river; *rere:* flowing. Flowing stream.

AWARIKI: *awa:* stream; *riki:* small. Small stream.

AWAROA: *awa:* river; *roa:* long. Long river.

AWARUA: *awa:* river; *rua:* two. Two rivers, or arms. The name is a common one in New Zealand and also throughout Polynesia. Avarua is the name of a harbour in Ra'iatea which had two openings in the reef.

AWATEA: Daylight, or midday.

AWATERE: *awa:* river; *tere:* swift flowing. Swift-flowing river. Of the river at East Cape it is said that in a battle one man had his stomach ripped open, and the contents ran swiftly down the current, hence the name.

The name may be the true form of Kawatiri, q.v.

AWATOITOI: *awa:* river; *toitoi:* a small fresh-water fish, a variety of flax, or possibly a corruption of *toetoe.*

AWATOTO: *awa:* river; *toto:* blood, or the name of a ceremony performed over a child, usually by the side of a stream.

AWATUNA: *awa:* creek; *tuna:* eel. Eel creek. The settlement of this name in Taranaki is known locally as Eels Creek.

AWHITU: Longing to return. Literally the meaning of *awhitu* is to feel regret for, to yearn for. At one time the Maoris at this settlement near the heads of the Manukau Harbour were forced to abandon their pa because of the depredations of the *taniwha* Kaiwhare, and they took the title Te Rua-o-Kaiwhare. It has been suggested that the place was named because of their longing to return to familiar surroundings and the place they loved.

E

EAHEINOMAUWE: This is Captain Cook's spelling of the Maori name for the North Island of New Zealand. It probably stands for *He ahi no Maui:* the fire of Maui, and refers to the volcanoes of the central plateau.

E KAPA: A modern name, after a Maori who lived here.

EKEMANUKA: *eke:* to crouch; *manuka:* tea-tree shrub. A party of Maoris who were out hunting saw a large enemy force approaching. They made their escape unseen by crouching down and creeping through the short manuka scrub.

EKETAHUNA: *eke:* to run aground; *tahuna:* shoal or sandbank. This place was as far as the Makakahi river could be navigated by canoes on account of the shoals.

EPUNI: Correctly Te Puni. He was the Ngati-Awa chief who greeted Wakefield and his companions when the *Tory* arrived off Petone beach. *E Puni!* is the vocative form of address, meaning O Puni!

ERUA: Two. The *e* is a particle used before digits one to nine in enumeration, e.g. *e rua, e toru,* two, three. Another ingenious explanation of the name has been offered in the form *E rua!* which could be translated colloquially, "Hullo, there's a cave!"

H

HAEHAENUI : *haehae:* to lacerate, or parallel grooves in a carving; *nui:* big. An ingenious but doubtful theory is that this is the original name for the Arrow River; it means "big scratches"—a reference to the number of channels the river has carved.

HAERE-HUKA : *haere:* to come or go; *huka:* foam. The name was apparently applied to the great rock in the middle of the rapids. It has been popularly translated Moving foam, or Flying foam.

HAIRINI : It has been stated several times that this is the Maori form of Ireland, but a more authoritative statement is that it is a missionary name, Cyrene, which takes this form in the Maori language.

HAKAHAKA : The name of a Marlborough chief.

HAKAKURA : *haka:* a South Island form of *whanga,* a hollow; *kura:* red. Reddish coloured hollow. It is the original Maori name for Lake Sumner.

HAKANA : This bay at Port Underwood is, in a roundabout way, probably named after the pioneer missionary, Rev. Samuel Ironside. He was known to the Maoris as Haeana, which was the nearest they could get to the pronunciation. Hakana is thought to be a corruption of Haeana.

HAKAPOUA : *haka:* South Island form of *whanga; poua:* old man. It is thought that the Maori used the expression "old man" in much the same way as the Pakeha might say "old man flood". The name has therefore been jocularly translated as Grandfather's Gully, Old Man Gulf, and Big Chasm of the Aged Man.

HAKAPUPU : *haka:* S.I. form of harbour; *pupu:* several kinds of shellfish. Estuary of the shellfish.

HAKA-PUREIREI : *haka:* dance; *pureirei:* tufts of grass, or small patch of garden.

HAKARU : *haka:* dance; *ru:* to shake.

HAKATARAMEA : *haka:* dance; *taramea:* spear-grass. The name commemorates a dance which took place near the mouth of the river. The performers wore bags filled with the sweet-scented gum from the flower stalks of the *taramea.* The bags in which the gum was contained were made of the skin of the *whekau,* an owl that is now extinct.

HAKATERE: *haka:* a form of *whaka,* to make; *tere:* swift. To make swift. It is the Maori name for the Ashburton River.

HAMAMA : to shout aloud. Three young men from Taumarunui came down the Whanganui River and killed a chief named Tama-tuna and insulted his wives. Tama-tuna was attacked unawares and in surprise he called out loudly.

HAMARIA : a missionary village on the shore of Lake Taupo which was named after the Biblical town of Samaria.

HAMURANA : The Maori form of the Biblical name Smyrna, given to the springs at Rotorua which were originally called Te Puna-a-Hangarua. See under Hangarua.

HANGAROA : An ornamental belt, anklet, or necklace made of shells.

HANGARUA : A name occasionally given to the Hamurana Springs, q.v. The full name is Te Puna-a-Hangarua, meaning The spring of Hangarua. It was presided over by a *taniwha* or water-monster named Hinerua. The small blind fish, *koaro,* which came up in the waters of the spring from time to time, were called the Children of Hinerua.

Tiki: greenstone image

HANGATIKI : *hanga:* to fashion or make; *tiki:* a grotesque image in human form. To carve a wooden post in the form of a tiki.

HAPARANGI : to shout or to cut open.

HAPUA : a hollow or pool.

HAPUAWHENUA: *hapua:* depression; *whenua:* land.

HAPUKU : the fish known to the Pakeha as groper.

HARAKEKE: flax (*Phormium tenax*).

HARIHARI : a song to make people pull together in unison.

HATAITAI : Many meanings are given for the name of this Wellington suburb. The most interesting is the myth that two taniwha once lived in the lake which is now Wellington Harbour. They attempted to force their way out. One of them, Ngake, succeeded, and made the entrance to the harbour. The other, Whataitai, failed. He changed into a bird and flew screaming to the top of Mount Victoria (Tangi-tekeo). The suburb should therefore be named Whataitai.

There have been attempts to provide a literal translation. *ha:* smell or breath (or *wha:* to cause or make known); *taitai:* tide, resulting in such meanings as The lapping of the tide, or The breath of the ocean.

HATEPE : to cut off, or to proceed in an orderly manner.

HATUMA : Possibly a personal name. It was sometimes called Whatuma. No meaning can be ascribed, but an old Maori once stated that it referred to the discoverers of the lake who ate until they were satisfied. The name was given by Tara.

HAUHANGAROA : *hau:* wind; *hangaroa:* sea-shells.

HAUMAITIKITIKI : Also in the form Haumatiketike it was applied to mountains such as Mount Brewster, Mount Prospect, and the Crown Range. The name is descriptive, meaning The wind blowing from the heights.

HAUMATAKITAKI : Named after a chieftainess of Otago.

HAUMOANA : *hau:* wind; *moana:* ocean. Sea breeze.

HAUNUI : *hau:* wind; *nui:* big. Strong wind.

HAUPAPA : *hau:* wind; *papa:* flat. Windy flat.

HAURAKI : *hau:* wind; *raki:* north. Northern wind. There is a proverb about Hauraki which refers to a wind that rises moaning from the sea. No doubt this is the north wind. It has been said, however, that Hauraki (or Haurangi) was a personal name.

HAUROKO : *hau:* wind; *roko:* South Island form of *rongo,* sound. Sound of the wind. This is the meaning ascribed to it by Southland Maoris, and the name has been officially noted as Hauroko. But it has been the subject of dispute in the past, for it is held by some northern Maoris that it should be Hauroto : *hau:* wind; *roto:* lake. Windy lake.

HAUTAPU : *hau:* there are many meanings. Here it may possibly refer to a religious ceremony; *tapu:* sacred. Sacred ceremony.

HAUTEKAPAKAPA: *hau:* wind; *te:* the; *kapakapa:* flapping. The flapping of the wind.

HAUTERE : *hau:* wind; *tere:* swift. Swift wind.

HAUTURU : *hau:* wind;

turu: post. Wind's resting-post. This is the Maori name for Little Barrier Island. In legend it is the centre post of the great net of Taramainuku. For an account of this net, see under Te Kupenga-a-Taramainuku.

HAUWAI : A mollusc.

HAWEA : The Hawea tribe was among the original inhabitants of the South Island. The lake and other places where the name occurs may be named originally from one of Rakai-haitu's men. If the name was given through some event in history, it implies doubt and indecision.

HAWERA : *ha:* breath; *wera:* hot, or burnt. Breath of fire. The occupants of a crowded whare were attacked by their enemies here, and the house was set on fire. The people who were inside were killed by "the breath of fire".

HE AHI NO MAUI : an ancient name for the north Island. See under Eaheino-mauwe.

HEIPIPI : *hei:* necklace; *pipi:* shell-fish. Necklace of pipis.

HEKEIA : The father of Te Anau, one of the early immigrants from Hawaiki.

HEKURA : The name of a woman of the Arai-te-uru canoe.

HEMO : to cease, or disappear.

HEREKINO : *here:* knot; *kino:* bad. Badly tied knot.

HERETAUNGA : *here:* to tie; *taunga:* to come to rest, applied to a canoe. But Heretaunga of the Hutt Valley was never a suitable place for canoes. It has been suggested that it is a corruption of Hautonga, breath of the south wind. There is also a theory that the name was imported from Hawke's Bay. The Heretaunga Plains were named after a notable carved house built near the present Hastings by Whatonga.

HIAPO : The famous sisters Kuiwai and Haungaroa left their brother Hiapo there while they went to Maketu to carry messages from Hawaiki to Ngatoro-i-rangi.

HIHITAHI : *hihi:* stitch-bird; *tahi:* single. A single stitch-bird.

HIKUAI : This may be a contraction of Hikuwai, one meaning of which is Tail end of the backwash. *hiku:* fish's tail; *wai:* water.

HIKURANGI : The name appears in many parts of New Zealand, because it commemorates a well-known and loved mountain peak in Hawaiki. The probable meaning is *hiku:*

point, or summit; *rangi:* sky.

HIKUTAIA : *hiku:* tail, or end; *taia:* neap tide. Tail end of the tide.

HIMATANGI : *hi:* to fish with hook and line; *Matangi:* the name of a chief. Matangi's fishing. At one time it was thought that the name was really Hima-tangi, referring to the weeping (*tangi*) of Hima for her lost greenstone treasure. But the story is now believed to relate to the chief Matangi who settled here long ago. Travellers were killed by a huge *taniwha* in a lake by the Manawatu River and Matangi set out with twelve men to kill it. Some of them acted as bait, tempting the *taniwha* from its home. Others lay in wait and snared it with ropes when it emerged, and killed it.

HINAHINA : a native tree.

HINAKURA : The name of a chieftainess who took ill and died by the Pahaoa River. She was buried there and the place was named after her. The true form of the name is Hinekura.

HINAU : a native tree.

HINERUA : *hine:* girl; *rua:* two. Two girls.

HINE-TE-AWA: *hine:* girl; *a:* of; *awa:* river. The girl of the river. This is the original name of Bowen Falls, which are named after a woman who lived long ago.

HINUERA: Properly Hinuwera. *hinu:* oil, or fat; *wera:* burning. Burning fat or oil.

HIONA : A missionary name for a pa on the Whanganui River. It is the Maori form of Zion.

HIRA : abundant, or multitude.

HIRUHARAMA : Maori form of Jerusalem. Named by the Rev. Richard Taylor.

HITAUA : a small waistmat or apron.

HIWINUI : *hiwi:* ridge; *nui:* big. Big ridge.

HIWIPANGO : Correctly Hiwiponga : *hiwi:* ridge; *ponga:* tree-fern. Ridge covered with tree-ferns.

HOE-O-TAINUI : *hoe:* paddle; *o:* of; *Tainui:* the Tainui canoe. Paddle of the Tainui canoe.

HOHONU : deep. A suitable name for the river.

HOKIANGA : It is from here that Kupe the navigator returned to Hawaiki. From this event the place was named Hokianga, Great returning place of Kupe. It is said that the proper form is Hoki-anga-nui (direct return), or Hokianga-nui-a-Kupe.

HOKIO : Whistling. Hau

gave the name because the wind whistled in his ears.

HOKITIKA : *hoki:* to return; *tika:* directly, or in a straight line. When some of the Ngai-Tahu were about to attack the pa here, one or more of their chiefs were drowned, and they therefore made a direct return back to their home. Long ago Bishop Harper wrote that the name means " 'When you get there, turn back again,' as the Maoris regard it as the end of the earth."

HOKONUI : There are two explanations. First, that *hoko* is a contraction of *hokowhitu:* war party; *nui:* large. Large war party. Second, that Hokonui is a corruption of *hukanui: huka:* snow; *nui:* big. Thick snow.

HOKOWHITU : war party of about 140 men. Hokowhitu near Palmerston North was so named because of the men who garrisoned at Te Motu-o-Poutoa.

HOMAI : to give to the person speaking.

HONGIHONGI : to smell. Turi of the Aotea canoe took up a handful of earth at this place and smelled it to see whether the soil was good.

HONGI'S POINT : The pa Kororipo where Hongi Hika carried the bodies of chiefs slain in battle was here.

HONGI'S TRACK : Where Hongi took his canoes overland in 1822 from Rotoehu to Rotoiti on his way to attack Mokoia · Island. The Maori name in Te Ara-a-Hongi.

HONIKIWI : *honi:* to nibble, or eat; *kiwi:* native flightless bird. Where the kiwi forages for food.

HORAHORA : greatly expanded, or scattered about.

HOREKE: to throw a spear.

HOROEKA : a native tree (lancewood).

HOROERA : *horo:* to swallow : *wera:* hot. To swallow hot.

HOROHORO : The name in full is Te Horohoroinga-o-nga-ringaringa-a-Tia, the place where Tia's hands were ceremoniously washed. This was necessary to remove the tapu after handling the dead. Tia was the Arawa explorer who named Lake Taupo.

An alternative for the full name is Te Horohoronga-a-Tia, which refers to the swallowing of sacred food in a ceremony to remove tapu.

HOROIRANGI : *horoi:* to wash, or cleanse; *rangi:* sky. When bad weather threatens Nelson, this mountain is covered with clouds.

HOROKIWI: *horo:* to run; *kiwi:* native bird. The running of the kiwi.

HOROKOAU: *horo:* to swallow; *koau:* shag. Te Horokoau is probably Mount Tasman, and is said to have been given this name because it resembled the swelling in the long neck of a shag when it is swallowing a fish. The name appears in several places in the South Island.

It is also the name for the Cass River, and could there be interpreted as A precipitous landslip (*horo*) where shags congregated.

HOROKOHATU: *horo:* crumbling; *kohatu:* stone. Crumbling stone. It may be an adaptation of the name Te Horokoatu, who was on the Arai-te-uru canoe.

HOROPITO: a native shrub (the pepper tree). The literal meaning is Scent of the woods.

HORORATA: *horo:* landslip; *rata:* native tree.

HOROTIU: *horo:* to run; *tiu:* swift. Swiftly flowing. Above the junction of the Waipa the Waikato River flowed swiftly. Until after the Waikato War the name Waikato was used only for the river below Ngaruawahia; above it was termed the Horotiu.

Hoteo: calabash

HOROTUTU: *horo:* landslip; *tutu:* native tree.

HOROWHENUA: *horo:* slip; *whenua:* land. Great landslide. The whole district from Levin to the Ohau River is a gravel deposit. It is a fan of detritus which has the appearance of an enormous landslide from the Tararuas.

HOTEO: a calabash.

HOUHORA: *hou:* feather; *hora:* to spread out. Feathers spread out. Feathers were at one time spread out near the Heads to dry.

HOUHOU: a native tree (five-finger).

HOUHOU-POUNAMU: *houhou:* to drill; *pounamu:* greenstone. To drill greenstone. This stream near Greytown was named from the custom of drilling greenstone and using the water of the stream in the process.

HOUIPAPA : *houi:* lacebark or ribbonwood tree; *papa:* flat. Ribbonwood flat. This is the name used by the Pakeha.

HOUPOTO : *hou:* feather; *poto:* short. Short feather.

HOUTO : ripe fruit of the poporo tree.

HUAPAI : *hua:* fruit; *pai:* good. Good fruit. This settlement was founded and named in 1912. It is a noted fruit-growing district.

HUARAU : *hua:* fruit; *rau:* hundred, or many. Plentiful fruit.

HUATAI : *hua:* product, or progeny; *tai:* tide. The name means Sea froth.

HUHUTAHI: *huhu:* thigh; *tahi:* single. Only thigh. One of Tama-tu-pere's thighs was eaten at this place, on which the settlement of Ranana was later established.

HUIA : an extinct bird, the feathers of which were greatly prized. It was never known to be in the Karamea district (the Huia River is a tributary of the Karamea). The name was probably conferred by an early surveyor.

HUIARAU : *huia:* extinct bird; *rau:* many. Many huia birds.

HUIHUI-KOURA : *hui-*

Huia: extinct bird

hui: assembly; *koura:* crayfish. Gathering of crayfish. Old Maoris tell stories of walls of crayfish plastered solidly several tiers deep in the waters of Stevens Island, in Breaksea Sound.

HUINGA : Said to mean swamps.

HUIROA : a species of fine flax.

HUI TE RĀNGIORA : name of the great explorer and navigator of the seventh century, who is reputed to have sailed down to the Antarctic in his canoe. The district adjoining the mouth of Motueka River was named after him.

HUKA : foam. The name of the great waterfall on the Waikato below Lake Taupo is Hukanui in full. Great body of foam.

HUKANUI : *huka:* foam, spray, or snow; *nui:* big.

HUKAPAPA : *huka:* snow, or frost; *papa:* flat. Frosty flat.

HUKARERE : *huka:* spray, or foam; *rere:* flying. Flying foam. This was the high seaward bluff of Scinde Island, Napier, and in storms the spray would come right to the hilltop at this point.

HUKERENUI : *hukere:* cascade; *nui:* big. Great cascade.

HUNUA : infertile, high country.

HURIAWA : *huri:* to turn round; *awa:* river. River turned round. The Waikouaiti River once entered the sea on the south side of the Huriawa Peninsula into Puketeraki Bay.

HURIMOANA : *huri:* to overflow; *moana:* ocean. Overflowing sea.

HURI-O-TE-WAI : *huri:* to turn round; *o:* of; *te:* the; *wai:* water. The dividing of the water. This is the Maori name of Bishop's Peninsula on Pepin Island, which diverts the Whakapuaka stream from the tide.

HURITINI : *huri:* to revolve; *tini:* many. Ever circling, or Many circles. It is a large pool of boiling muddy water at Tikitere, and is therefore a descriptive name.

HURUHURU - O - TAI - KAWA : *huruhuru:* coarse hair; *o:* of; *Taikawa:* name of a chieftainess. The local meaning, however, is The soft hair of Taikawa. She insisted that the *muka* or dressed flax of this part of Horowhenua was so fine that it should be called by this name.

HURUNUI : *huru:* hair; *nui:* big. One explanation is that the name means Flowing hair. It does have something of this appearance from the hills. It may have taken its name from the female dog, Hurunui, which Kupe was supposed to have left in charge of his discoveries. It may also refer to vegetation by the banks.

I

IHU-NGAU-ANA : *ihu:* nose. Nose bitten off. A chief named Tama-haki had his nose bitten off by Kura at a battle at this place on the Whanganui River.

IKAMATUA : *ika:* fish; *matua:* parent, or fully grown. One explanation of the name is that it is a shortened form of Te Ika-a-matua, The fish of my ancestor (Maui).

IKORAKI : a South Island form of Hikurangi, q.v.

INANGAHUA : *inanga:* whitebait; *hua:* preserved by drying in the sun, or plenty of. The Inangahua River was noted for the big catches of whitebait that it yielded.

IRIMAHUWHERI : The correct name of this headland in the Buller district is Irimahuwhero. *iri:* hanging; *mahu:* hair; *whero:* red. Hanging red hair. On the seaward side of the headland there are masses of rata trees which are sometimes ablaze with red blooms.

IWIKATEA : *iwi:* bone; *katea:* bleached. Bleached bones. This is the Maori name for the site of Balclutha. A great battle took place there long ago, and the bones remained for many years.

IWIRUA : *iwi:* bone; *rua:* pit, or cave. There may have been a burial ground on this cape in Grove Arm, Marlborough Sounds.

IWITUAROA : backbone. From the sea the Iwituaroa Range bears a striking resemblance to a human backbone.

K

KAEO : freshwater shellfish.

KAHAROA : *kaha:* net; *roa:* long. Large seine or dragnet.

KAHIKA : native tree, white pine. Short for Kahikatea.

KAHIKATEA : white pine.

Kahikatea Bay was an early name for Curious Cove.

KAHINU : This peak in the Tararuas was named after a chief of the Rangitane pa.

KAHIWIROA : *kahiwi:* ridge; *roa:* long. Long ridge.

KAHU : Named after Kahumata-momoe, son of Tama-te-kapua, because he stayed here at Orakei in Auckland.

KAHUI : flock, or herd.

KAHUIKA : the meeting of the waters. It is the equivalent of the North Island Ngahuinga, and is a descriptive name, for it is at the meeting of the Matau and Clutha Rivers.

KAHUI-KAKAPO : *kahui:* meeting; *kakapo:* ground parrot. "Kakapo Parliament". An old legend says that Doubtful Sound was a place where the chief of the kakapo sent out invitations to his subjects to meet together to discuss matters of common interest among the parrots. Spey River and Hall's Arm were similar meeting places.

KAHUI-KAU-PEKA : assembly of river-heads. The Maori name for D'Archiac, which is the source of many rivers.

KAHUI-KAWAU : *kahui:* assembly; *kawau:* shag. Assembly of shags. Ihenga's wife exclaimed with delight at the many birds he had brought in his canoe, so the place, between Rotorua and Maketu, was given this name.

KAHUITAMARIKI : *kahui:* assembly; *tamariki:* grandchildren. Assembly of grandchildren.

KAHUKURA : rainbow, or god of the rainbow.

KAHURANAKI : Properly Kahura-a-nake, the wished for. When the Maoris set out from Wairoa to Ahuriri in their canoes, this high hill was their landmark. If it became obscured by clouds, it was greatly wished for.

KAHURANGI : *kahu:* blue; *rangi:* sky. Blue skies. Canoe voyagers from the North Island, Nelson and Marlborough always endeavoured to reach the mouth of the Kahurangi River in the evening, because this landfall was almost invariably associated with blue skies and calm waters.

KAHUTARA : the name of one of the canoes in which the Maoris came to New Zealand. The Ngai-Tahu came from the North Island in a canoe with the same name and established themselves here, a little south of Kaikoura.

KAHUWERA : *kahu:* garment; *wera:* burnt. Burnt garment. The Maori village in the Bay of Islands was so named because a woman's garment caught fire here, and she had to rush into the sea to extinguish it. The same name in Southland comes from the name of a woman who lived there about three hundred years ago.

KAIAKA : adept, or man.

KAIAPOI : It is generally agreed that the proper form of the name is Kaiapohia, meaning food depot. But some South Island Maoris deny this, and say that it has always been Kaiapoi. *Kai:* food; *poi:* swung. The pa was in a strategic position and adequate food supplies could be "swung" towards it from all directions.

KAIARERO : *kai:* to bite, or eat; *arero:* tongue. Bite the tongue.

KAIATA : *kai:* food; *ata:* morning. Eat in the morning.

KAIATE : *kai:* food; *ate:* liver. Meal of liver. The livers of sharks were often eaten here.

KAIAUA : *kai:* to eat; *aua:* herring. Meal of herring.

KAI-HAU-O-KUPE : *kai:* eating; *hau:* wind; *o:* of; Kupe. Kupe's wind-eating. This spot at Castlecliff is a place where Kupe stayed at a time that it was very windy.

KAIHERE: *kai:* food; *here:* to tie.

KAIHIKU: *kai:* to eat; *hiku:* tail of a fish. To eat fish tails.

KAIHINU: *kai:* food; *hinu:* fat. Rich food.

KAIHU: The full name was Kai-hu-a-Ihenga. *kai:* food; *hu:* secret; *a:* of; *Ihenga:* grandson of Tama-te-kapua. He went travelling in the far north, and his men carried some toheroa inland. While his companions were absent, he ate all the remaining supplies, and pretended he knew nothing about it. He was found out, and the place named as a reminder of his greed.

KAI-IWI: *kai:* number; *iwi:* tribe. Gathering of the tribes. Several meanings have been advanced. *Kai* also means eat, and *iwi* means bone. One of the stories is that a chief ate the flesh and bones of birds; and another is that food of bone was threat against an enemy tribe. It is also said that a woman named Hine-koatu was killed and eaten, and her bones thrown into the stream. And there is an amusing tale that a woman named Kiteiwi was one day eating a choice morsel of *kuia* (old woman). Someone asked her what she was eating, and she replied, "The bone of a *kokako* (New Zealand crow)", which was a good joke, and so the place was named Kai-iwi (eat the bone).

KAIK: village. This name, which occurs often in the South Island, is the same as the North Island *kainga,* an unfortified village.

KAIKANOHI: *kai:* to eat; *kanohi:* eye. A noted warrior caught his wife with another man and swallowed her eyes as an act of revenge. Thus a point on Ellesmere Spit gained its name. Elsewhere in the South Island the name came from unworked greenstone, and was also the name of a famous *mere* (club).

KAIKANUI: *kaika:* village (*kainga*); *nui:* big. Big settlement.

KAIKOHE: *kai:* food; *kohe:* tree, or climbing plant.

KAIKORAI: Properly Kaikarae. *kai:* to eat; *karae:* a sea bird.

KAIKOURA: *kai:* to eat; *koura:* crayfish. To eat crayfish. The full name is Te Ahi-kai-koura-a-Tama-ki-te-rangi (or Tamatea-pokai-whenua). This great traveller stayed here and lit a fire to cook a meal of crayfish, and this is what the full name means. The name of this place was once applied to the whole of the South Island.

KAIMAI : *kai:* to eat; *mai:* mussel. To eat mussels.

KAIMANAWA : *kai:* to eat; *manawa:* heart. Heart-eater.

KAIMATA : *kai:* to eat; *mata:* unripe, or uncooked. To eat raw food.

KAIMATAITAI : *kai:* to eat; *mataitai:* salty. Salty food.

KAIMATUHI : *kai:* to eat; *matuhi:* bush wren. To eat matuhi.

KAIMAUMAU : *kai:* food; *maumau:* wasted. Wasted food.

KAIMIRO : *kai:* to eat; *miro:* native tree. To eat miro berries.

KAIMOKO : a man skilled in the art of tattooing. This operation was probably carried out alongside the stream.

KAINAMU : *kai:* to eat; *namu:* sandfly. To eat sandflies. At this place on the Waiau River a Maori was plagued by sandflies. He licked his hand to allay the itching and inadvertently secured a mouthful of them.

KAINGAROA : *kainga:* meal; *roa:* long. Protracted meal. The name in full is Te Kaingaroa-a-Haungaroa. A priestess named Haungaroa was exploring the plains. She took so long over her meal that she was teased by her companions, and the place was called The long meal of Haungaroa. The women who made the remark were changed into cabbage trees which recede across the plain before travellers.

KAIPAKATITI: *kai:* food; *pakatiti:* defective. Inedible food.

KAIPAKIRIKIRI : *kai:* food; *pakirikiri:* rock-cod. Rock-cod food.

KAIPARA : *kai:* to eat; *para:* fern-root. To eat fern-root. When Kahu-mata-momoe and his nephew Ihenga were visiting here, they were well fed, and amongst the food there was a basket of *para.* They had never seen or tasted

Matuhi: bush wren

34

it before, and named the place after the meal.

KAIPARA-TE-HAU: Properly Kapara-te-hau. *Kapara:* to sport; *te:* the; *hau:* wind. The wind is sporting. The name probably comes from the chief Te Hau who was offended by Kupe, who caused the area to be inundated by the sea. It is the shallow lake or lagoon which later became Lake Grassmere.

KAIPARORO: *kai:* to eat; *paroro:* bad weather. To eat bad weather. There is a flat-topped hill, and the fogs disappear when they reach it.

KAIPIPI: *kai:* to eat; *pipi:* shell-fish. To eat pipis.

KAIPO: *kai:* to eat; *po:* night. To eat at night.

KAIPUKE: *kai:* to eat; *puke:* hill. The hill that was eaten. In the old whaling days several ships set out their sails to dry by Kororareka Point, thus obscuring the hill. Quick to make a joke, the Maoris called it Kaipuke.

KAIPURUA: *kai:* food; *purua:* done in pairs. Fish caught in pairs. A Maori who was fishing in this tributary of the Waiau caught two fish simultaneously.

KAIRANGA: a company of men making a charge in battle.

KAIRARA: *kai:* food; *rara:* spread out on a platform. Food spread out on a stage.

KAIREPEREPE: *kai:* to eat; *reperepe:* elephant-fish. Meal of elephant-fish.

KAIRUA: A contraction of Kopukairua. *kopu:* full; *kai:* food; *rua:* pit. Well-stocked food pit.

KAITAIA: In full, Kaitataia. *kai:* food; *tataia:* thrown about. Two women competed to see who could store away the most food. Eventually there was so much gathered together that it could not be contained in the store-pits and had to be thrown away.

There is another legend to the effect that Tamatea, son of Rongokako, took vast quantities of wood-pigeons here. The name of the place was changed from Orongotea to Kaitaia (food in abundance).

KAITAKATA: a South Island form of Kaitangata, man-eater. A party of Maoris travelling along the beach near Orepuki were overwhelmed by a "man-eating" wave.

KAITANGATA: *kai:* to eat; *tangata:* man. The eating of man. After a battle between two tribes over eeling rights on the lakes, the chief Mokomoko was eaten by his victors.

Another account says that the place was named after one

of the crew of the Arai-te-uru canoe who found a supply of paint in the hills nearby, and was skilled at using it.

KAITANGIWEKA : *kai:* food; *tangi:* to cry; *weka:* wood-hen. The crying of the wood-hen for food.

KAI-TARAKIHI : *kai:* food; *tarakihi:* native fish. Meal of tarakihi. The fishing ground is located by the Maoris by sailing out until this mountain comes into view.

KAITAWA : *kai:* to eat; *tawa:* native tree.

KAITERETERE : *kai:* to eat; *teretere:* quickly. To eat in a hurry. Local Maoris who were having a meal on the beach were surprised by stones which rolled down the hillside. Fearing a surprise attack, they gathered their food together and ate hurriedly as they retired to the pa.

KAITI : *kai:* to eat; *ti:* cabbage tree. To eat the leaves of the cabbage tree.

KAITIEKE : *kai:* to eat; *tieke:* saddle-back. To eat the saddle-back (native bird).

KAITOKE : *kai:* to eat; *toke:* worm. The soil was very poor, and on occasion nothing could be found to eat but worms.

KAITORETE : *kai:* to eat; *torete:* parakeet. To eat parakeet. The Ellesmere Spit was a place that had a plentiful supply of birds and fish for food.

KAITUNA : *kai:* to eat; *tuna:* eel. To eat eels. There were many localities with this name, and no doubt it was a sign that eels abounded, and were a popular food.

KAIUKU : *kai:* to eat; *uku:* blue clay. To eat clay. The people of this pa were beleagured, and when their food supplies ran out, they ate clay to assuage their hunger. Their bravery and tenacity was rewarded when a *taua* came to their aid, the warriors being pulled up the cliff to the pa by ropes.

KAIUMU : *kai:* food; *umu:* oven. Food oven.

KAIWAIWAI : Correct spelling Kaiwaewae. *kai:* to eat; *waewae:* foot. Destructive to the feet. In the early days the wild Irishman shrub grew plentifully round about Featherston, and took toll of the bare feet of the Maoris.

KAIWAKA : *kai:* to eat; *waka:* canoe. Destroyer of canoes. Most places where this name is found are by banks of a swiftly-running river or stream which is noted for the canoes "eaten" or destroyed.

KAIWHARAWHARA: *kai:*

to eat; *wharawhara:* fruit of the astelia which grows in the forks of trees. To eat *wharawhara*.

KAKA : native parrot.

KAKAHI : fresh-water mussel.

KAKAHO : culm of the *toetoe* grass.

KAKAHOROA : *kakaho:* culm of the *toetoe; roa:* long. The original name for Whakatane.

KAKANUI: Properly Kakaunui. *kakau:* to swim, or stalk of plant; *nui:* many. Many plant stalks, or swimming or crossing a river.

KAKAPO : ground parrot.

KAKAPUAKA : *kaka:* parrot; *kuaka:* dry twigs or flowers.

Kakariki: N.Z. parakeet

KARARAMEA : A contraction of Kakara taramea. Scent made from gum extracted from the leaves of spear grass. See under Karamea.

KAKARIKI : parakeet.

KAKATAHI: *kaka:* parrot; *tahi:* single. One parrot.

KAKEPUKU : Correctly, and in full, Kakipuku-o-Kahurere. *kaki:* neck; *puku:* swollen. The name was given hundreds of years ago by Rakataura, partly after his wife Kahurere, and partly because of the shape of the hill near Te Awamutu. It is also said that the full name is Kakepuku-te-aroaro-o-Kahukeke.

KAKIROA : *kaki:* neck; *roa:* long. The name of a Waitaha ancestor, or one of the crew of the Arai-te-uru.

Kaka: New Zealand parrot

KA - KOHAKA - RURU - WHENUA: In standard Maori the name would appear as Nga - kohanga - ruru - whenua. *nga:* the; *kohanga:* nest; *ruruwhenua:* large owl, or morepork. The nests of the large owls. Some southern Maoris went up to Moonlight Gully in the early sixties to dig for gold, and cooked and ate these owls, giving this name to what later became Moonlight Gully.

KAMAHI : a native tree.

KAMAKA : rock or stone.

KAMAUTURUA: the fastening of two bundles. The name of a chief of the Arai-te-uru canoe was given to the Burnett Range.

KAMO : to bubble up. Descriptive of the hot springs.

KAMOKAMO : winking. When the chief Porourangi was murdered, winking was adopted as a signal for setting upon him.

KANAPA : shining.

KANIERE : the act of sawing greenstone.

KANOHI : eye, or face.

KA-PAKIHI-WHAKATE-KATEKA-A-WAITAHA: *ka:* the; *pakihi:* open grass country; *whakatekateka:* to play with a dart; *a:* of; *Waitaha:* a tribe. The open grass country where the Waitaha people would have room to play the game of throwing darts. It is a very old name for the Canterbury Plains, and there is an inference that there was no room for such sport in the hills and gullies of Otago.

KAPITI : Short for Ko-te-waewae - kapiti - o - Tara - raua - ko-Rangitane, the place where the boundaries of Tara and Rangitane divide.

KAPONGA : a tree-fern.

KAPOUPOU - O - TE - RA - KIHOUIA : the posts of Raki-houia. He was the son of Rakaihaitu, who dug the southern lakes. Rakihouia made a number of eel-weirs, and this very old name for Canterbury coast was received because of the posts he planted in the rivers in order to make eel-weirs.

KAPO-WAIRUA : *kapo:* snatching; *wairua:* soul. A place where demons snatch at the spirits of the dead in Tom Bowling Bay as they pass to the afterlife.

KAPUARANGI : *kapua:* cloud; *rangi:* sky. Cloudy sky.

KAPUKA : a native tree.

KAPUKA - TAU - MOHA - KA : snaring pigeons with a string. A name which describes pigeon-hunting on the slopes of Mount Cargill.

KA - PUKE - MAEROERO : *ka (nga):* the; *puke:* hill;

maeroero : wild men of the hills. The hills of the wild men. This was the Maori name for the foothills of the Southern Alps.

KAPUNI : an assembly. A place named by Turi of the Aotea canoe where he and his men camped by a river.

KARAKA : a native tree.

KARAMEA : A shortened form of Kakara-taramea : *ka kara:* scent; *taramea:* speargrass. The scent was made from the gum extracted from the leaves of the spear-grass. The *kakara taramea* made by the women of the Karamea district was highly valued, and Maoris came from long distances to barter food and greenstone for it.

KARAMU : a native shrub.

KARANGAHAKE : *karanga:* to welcome; *hake:* hunchback. Loosely translated as a Meeting of the hunchbacks, a phrase which is descriptive of the cluster of low hills in the vicinity.

KARANGAHAPE : a shellfish. There is a story that a hill on the East Coast was called Karanga - na - Hape, because the chief Hape pursued a wounded moa up a hillside. He attacked it with his *taiaha* (weapon), but it kicked him, and his leg was broken, and he rolled down the hill.

KARANGARUA: *karanga:* to call; *rua:* two.

KARAPIRO : *kara:* stone; *piro:* stinking.

KARAPIṬI : to fasten, or place side by side.

KARATIA : Maori form of Galatia, a missionary settlement on the Whanganui River, originally called Hikurangi.

KAREKARE : surf.

KARETU : sweet - scented grass.

KARIOI : to loiter. A place where the Maoris sometimes lingered.

KARIRI : Maori form of Galilee. Early mission station.

KARITANE : *kari:* to dig; *tane:* men. Men digging. This may be a reference to the digging of a ditch to catch eels. Another explanation is that while the Huriawa pa was being besieged, some of the men slipped out on a fishing expedition leaving only the wounded *(kari)* to defend the pa.

KARORI: In full, Te-kaha-o-nga-rore, The rope of the snares. Before European settlement the Karori valley was noted for its birds.

KARORO : The proper name is Kararoa. *kara:* beach; *roa:* long. Long shelving beach.

KARTIGI : Properly Katiki. *Ka (nga):* the; *tiki:* carved figure. The tikis.

39

KARU-MOE-RANGI : to day-dream.

KATIKATI : nibbling. In full, Katikati - o - Tama - te - kapua, The nibbling of Tama-te-kapua. When they reached this place, Tama-te-kapua's men ate their food quickly, but the captain of the Arawa canoe kept nibbling his, hence the name.

KATIPO: a small venomous spider.

KAUAERANGA : no crossing here.

KAUANA : Maori form of the name Cowan, who was an early settler in the Oreti River basin.

KAU-ARA-PAOA : *kau:* to swim; *ara:* path; *Paoa (Pawa):* the route by which Pawa swam across the river. Pawa was Kupe's servant. He went up the Whanganui River, and Pawa swam to the other side to get some *korau* (native turnip) and was drowned. This was an important place because here Kupe heard voices. They were the voices of the weka, kokako, and tiwaiwaka. When he found they were birds and not men, this early explorer returned to the mouth of the river.

KAUKAPAKAPA : *kau:* to swim; *kapakapa:* flapping. To swim with much splashing. There were wild ducks in the creek, and they were chased away or hunted with much flapping of their wings.

KAUKAU : Corrupt form of Kaka, parrot.

KAUNGAROA : Properly Kauangaroa. *kauanga:* ford; *roa:* long. Long ford.

KAURI : Short for Kauri-hohore, a bald or smooth-barrelled kauri tree.

KAUROA : *kau:* to swim; *roa:* long. To swim for a long time.

KAUWAE WHAKATO-RO: *kauwae:* jaw; *whakatoro:* to stretch out. The Ngai-tahu tribe, fighting against the Ngati-mamoe, sent out decoys at Hillend. Then they closed round their victims like jaws round food.

Kauri: New Zealand pine

KAWAKAWA: a native tree. Kawakawa at East Cape is in full Te Kawakawa-mai-tawhiti, and has come from Hawaiki.

KAWARAU: *kawa:* shrub; *rau:* many. Many shrubs.

KAWATIRI: There are many explanations of the meaning of the Maori name of the Buller River, some of which are lengthy. A noted authority believed that it should really have been Ko Awatere, The swift river.

KAWAU: shag.

KAWERAU: *kawe:* to carry; *rau:* many. Many carriers. The district was first settled by the Tini-o-Kawe-rau tribe from Hawaiki, which took its name from a chief.

KAWHIA: In full, Ka-awhia. The name was given by Turi of the Aotea canoe when he entered the harbour. An *awhiawhi* was a ceremony performed on entering a new land to protect the explorers from evil influences. Each phrase of the *karakia* (chant) that Turi used began with *ka.*

KAWITI: the Maori chief who fought against the British forces in the Bay of Islands.

KEKERENGU: black beetle. The name comes from a young Maori chief who had to flee to this place because of the enmity of Rangihaeata.

KENANA: Maori form of Canaan.

KENEPURU: sandy silt.

KEREPEHI: clod of earth. An old Maori said that it was a clod of earth, "easy to hold".

KERIKERI: to keep on digging.

KETEKETERAU: *kete-kete:* to click the tongue; *rau:* many. Many clickings of the tongue. Tara, son of Whatonga, set out to avenge the killing of his dog. He landed at what was then the outlet of the Ahuriri lagoon, Napier, and jumped ashore. Then he remembered he had left his *putatara* (trumpet) at Wairoa, and gave vent to his surprise by many clickings of his tongue.

KETEMARAE: *kete:* kit; *marae:* courtyard. Basket on the marae. An old woman at the pa on the site of Norman-by had only one basket of food to give to visitors. She put it on the *marae.*

KETETAHI: *kete:* basket; *tahi:* one. One basket.

KIEKIE: a native vine.

KIHIKIHI: cicada. An onomatopœic name.

KIKOWHAKARERE: *kiko:* body; *whakarere:* cast away. Bodies cast away. The

Kete: basket

Maoris of Whangapoua surprised those at Kikowhakarere, but were defeated. They had to leave so many behind who were dead or wounded, that the place received its name.

KILMOG : A whaler's pronunciation of *kirimoho:* a species of *manuka,* or tea-tree. It was used to make an infusion of tea.

KIMIAKAU : *kimi:* to look for; *akau:* coast. To look for the coast. A band of explorers followed the course of the Arrow River to see if they could find a way through to the west coast.

KIMIHIA : to seek.

KINOHAKU : *kino:* bad, or ugly; *haku:* kingfish.

KIOKIO : a native fern.

KIORE : native rat.

KIOREROA : *kiore:* rat; *roa:* long. Long rat.

KIRIKAU : *kiri:* skin; *kau:* bare. Naked. A battle in which the contestants were naked was fought here long ago.

KIRIKIRI-KATATA: *kiri-kiri:* a mass of rock; *katata:* sharp points. A sharp-pointed mass of rock. The Maori name for Mount Cook.

KIRIKIRIROA : *kirikiri:* gravel; *roa:* long. Long stretches of gravel. The Maori name for Hamilton.

KIRIKOPUNI : dark-skinned eel.

KIRIOHINEKAI : the skin of Hinekai. It was a hot pool at Rotorua which was useful in the cure of skin diseases.

KIRIPAKA : quartz, or flint.

KIRITAKI : to pull off the bark. There was a totara tree from which a great deal of bark was taken.

KIWI : flightless bird.

KIWITAHI : *kiwi:* bird; *tahi:* one. Single kiwi.

KIWITEA : *kiwi:* bird; *tea:* white. White kiwi.

KOHAI : a form of *kowhai,* flowering tree.

KOHANGA : nest.

KOHEKOHE : a native tree.

KOHI : seasick. When the Mataatua canoe paddled towards the shore in the Bay of Plenty, the ground-swell made Wairaka, the daughter of Toroa, sick.

KOHIMARAMA: *kohi:* point; *marama:* light. Light on a headland.

KOHUA-ORA: cooked in an earth oven while alive It refers to an event of long ago at Papatoetoe.

KOHUKETE: *kohu:* mist; *kete:* basket. Mist in the form of a basket. The chief Koha took this form of mist as the sign of an approaching enemy.

KOHUKOHU: moss, seaweed, a plant, or a tree.

KOHUMARU: *kohu:* mist; *maru:* sheltered. Sheltered from the fog.

KOHUNUI: *kohu:* mist; *nui:* big. Big mist, or ground mist.

KOHURATAHI: *kohura:* to sprout; *tahi:* single.

KOHUTAI: *kohu:* mist; *tai:* tide. Sea foam.

KOIRO: conger eel.

KOKAKO: native crow.

KOKAKORIKI: *kokako:* crow; *riki:* little, or few. Few kokakos.

KOKIRI: to dash forward, or charge.

KOKONGA: angle or corner. The name probably comes from the bend in the river.

KOKOPU: small freshwater fish.

KOKORI: a small bay.

KOKOWAI: red earth,

Ko: digging implement

from which red ochre was obtained by burning.

KOMATA: end of a range of hills.

KONGAHU: boulders. There are many boulders in this part of the Buller district.

KONINI: fruit of native fuchsia.

KOPAKI: to wrap.

KOPI-O-KAITANGATA: *kopi:* gorge; *o:* of; *kaitangata:* man-eater. Cannibal gorge. Parties of Maoris travelled to the west coast through this gorge, their passage being marked by cannibal feasts. An alternative name is Kapai-o-kaitangata, Good feed of human flesh.

KOPU: a deep hole in a river.

KOPUA: deep.

KOPUARAHI: *kopua:* deep pool; *rahi:* large. Large deep hole.

KOPUARANGA: *kopua:* deep hole; *ranga:* shoal of fish. Fish in a deep pool.

KOPUAWHARA: *kopua:* deep pool; *whara:* plant. Deep pool with astelia growing round it.

KOPUKU: closely woven cloak.

KOPURIKI: *kopu:* belly; *riki:* little. Little stomach.

KOPUREHEREHE: *kopu:* belly; *reherehe:* wrinkled. The name refers to eels which had been fat, but had become shrunk and wrinkled.

KOPURIKI: *kopu:* small fish; *riki:* few. Hardly any fish.

KOPUTAI: high tide. Some Maoris landed at Port Chalmers and went soundly to sleep.

Kopuku: cloak

When they woke they found that their canoes had drifted away on the tide. They shouted "Koputai!" (High tide!).

KOPUTAROA: *koputa:* snare for catching parakeets; *roa:* long. Long snare.

KOPUTAUAKI: to relax comfortably after a feast, which was exactly what happened after a cannibal banquet.

KOPUTIRAHA: Lying back with the arms above the head. An attitude adopted by a chief at this place, which is now the business centre of Nelson.

KORAKONUI: *korako:* albino; *nui:* big. Big albino.

KORANUI: Short for Koro-koronui. *Korokoro:* throat; *nui:* big. Big throat. The valley is long and narrow and may be said to resemble a throat.

KOREKE: quail.

KORERE: channel.

KORINITI: Maori form of Corinth. A missionary settlement on the Whanganui River.

KORITO: unexpanded leaves, or a variety of greenstone.

KOROKATA: Maori form of Golgotha. Te Rauparaha raided this place, just outside Whanganui, and fourteen years later the Rev. Richard Taylor was so horrified by the number

44

of human bones to be seen there that he called the place Golgotha.

KOROKORO : throat.

KOROMIKO : native veronica.

KORORAREKA : *korora:* blue penguin; *reka:* sweet, or tasty. An old chief lay dying and expressed a wish for a penguin. After much searching one was found. When it was cooked he was too weak to eat it, but he drank some of the water in which it had been boiled, and murmured, "Ka reka te korora!" (How sweet is the penguin!)

KORU : to fold, or folded.

KO - TE - KETE - IKA - A - TUTEKAWA: the fish basket of Tutekawa. A proverb which applied to Lakes Forsyth and Ellesmere because they were so full of fish.

KOTEMAORI : Incorrect form of Te Moari, the giant swing.

KOTINGA : boundary line.

KOTUKU : white heron. It is an abbreviation of the Maori name for Lake Brunner, Kotuku-whakaoka. *Whakaoka:* to stab. The reference is to the kotuku darting its long, sharp beak down to catch fish. Another name for Lake Brunner is Kotuku-moana.

KOUKOU - PARATA :

tame owl. Maori name for Port Levy.

KOURA : crayfish.

KOURARIKI : whale-feed. Maori name for Cape Providence.

KOUTU : promontory. A descriptive name.

KOWAI : shortened form of Kowhai, flowering tree.

KOWHAI : flowering tree.

KOWHATU : stone.

KUAOTUNA:*kuao:*young; *tuna:* eel. Young of eels.

KUIRAU : *kui:* old woman; *rau:* many. A picnic spot at Rotorua where the old women cooked the *kai* (food).

KUMARA : sweet potato. Kumara on the West Coast however was named after a flower, either of the convolvulus, or the bush-lawyer. It may originally have been *kohimara.*

KUMEROA : *kume:* to pull; *roa:* long. A long pull.

KUMEU : *kume:* to pull; *u:* breast. Pulling the breasts. This is probably an action similar to that performed by Ruataupere of Ngati-Porou. To incite a war party to avenge her cousin's death, she bared her bosom and pulled her breasts.

KUPENGA-A-KUPE : *kupenga:* net; *a:* of; *Kupe:* the famous explorer. Kupe left a

45

net here at Jackson's Head as a sign of his having been there.

KURIPUNI : *kuri:* native dog; *puni:* place of encampment.

KURIWAO : *kuri:* dog; *wao:* bush. Wild dog.

KUROW : Correctly Kohurau. *Kohu:* mist; *rau:* many. Many fogs. The name probably came originally from one of the crew of the Arai-te-uru.

KUWHA-RUA-O-KAHU : As Kahu-mata-mamoe went ashore at Lake Rotoiti, he threw off his clothes. His grandsons laughed and shouted, "Ho! Ho! see, there go Kahu's legs!" and so the place was named.

M

MAENENE : smooth.

MAEREWHENUA : Possibly this should be Maerowhenua. *maero:* original inhabitants; *whenua:* land. Land of the wild men, or strange folk. An alternative meaning and spelling could be Maruwhenua; *maru:* shelter. The name is applied to the rock shelters with their unusual Maori paintings near Duntroon.

MAERO : wild men.

MAHAKI : mild, or calm.

MAHAKIPAWA : *mahaki:* calm; *pawa:* smoke. When Te Rauparaha raided the valley, the inhabitants saw him coming and set fire to their pa. Te Rauparaha saw the smoke rising calmly in the air, and said, "I see smoke!"

MAHANA : warm.

MAHARAHARA : to keep in remembrance another's fault.

MAHAU : shelter.

MAHENO : island. The name was conferred by a Pakeha.

MAHEPUKU : a rounded sinker. The Maori name for Pepin Island.

MAHIA : to sound, or resound. The Mahia Peninsula was named Te Mahia-mai-Tawhiti after a place in Tahiti.

MAHINAHINA : refers to grey hair.

Mahau: porch

46

MAHINAPUA : *Mahina:* proper name; *pua:* flower. Mahina's flower.

MAHITAHI : Properly Maitahi. *mai:* garment; *tahi:* one. Single garment.

MAHOE : a native tree.

MAHOENUI: *mahoe:* tree; *nui:* big, or plenty of. Many mahoe trees.

MAHOETAHI : *mahoe:* tree, *tahi:* single. Single mahoe tree.

MAHUNUI : the name of the canoe in which Maui came to New Zealand. This canoe was the South Island, Te Waka-a-Maui, from which he fished up (discovered) Te Ika-a-Maui, the North Island. Also Maahunui.

MAHURANGI : One of the explanations of the name is that the Tainui canoe called in here before the portage over the Tamaki Isthmus, and that this place, later known as Warkworth, was so-called after the chieftainess who designed the Tainui canoe in Hawaiki.

MAHUTA : Named after the third Maori King, son of Tawhiao.

MAIA : brave.

MAIKI : the high place. The peak where the flagstaff stands at Russell.

MAIMAI : The place of this name in Westland is not a Maori word, but a corruption of the Australian word for a rough camp or bivouac, brought over by the gold-diggers.

MAIRANGI : shortened form of Omairangi, the place of Mairangi.

MAIRE-KURA : *maire:* native tree; *kura:* red garment. Red garment hanging on a maire tree. A chief dared his enemies to cross the Whanganui River by hanging his red garment in a tree.

MAIROA: *mai:* mussels out of their shells; *roa:* many.

MAITAI : The proper spelling is Maitahi, and refers to one particular matai or mai (black pine) which grew on the bank of the river.

MAKAHU : *ma:* white; *kahu:* hawk. White hawk.

MAKARA : head, or to come or go.

MAKARAKA : *ma* (short for *manga*) : stream; *karaka:* native tree. A place where karaka trees grew by a stream.

MAKARAU : *maka:* to throw; *rau:* to catch in a net.

MAKARETU : *ma:* stream; *karetu:* sweet-scented grass. Stream where the sweet-scented grass grows.

MAKAREWA : *maka:* fish-hook; *rewa:* floating. Fish-hooks floating on the water.

After baiting hooks to catch eels, the local Maoris found them floating on the surface of the water after a storm.

MAKARINI: named for Sir Donald McLean.

MAKARORA: *maka* (S.I. form of *manga*): stream; *rora:* spread out.

MAKARORE: *maka:* part of a bird snare; *rore:* to ensnare.

MAKATOTE: *ma:* stream; *katote:* tree-fern. Tree-ferns growing by a stream.

MAKAURI: *ma:* stream; *kauri:* native tree. Kauris growing by a stream.

MAKAWHIO: *ma:* stream; *whio:* blue duck. Stream of the blue duck.

MAKERONIA: Maori form of Macedonia. The pa was built at the time of the Hauhau wars.

MAKERIKERI: *ma:* stream; *kerikeri:* rushing violently. Turbulent stream.

MAKETU: named after a place in Hawaiki.

MAKIEKIE: *ma:* stream; *kiekie:* native flower plant. Stream where the *kiekie* grows.

MAKIKIHI: *ma:* stream; *kikihi:* cicada. Stream of the cicadas. Or *kikihi* may refer to the sound of the cicadas, in which case the meaning is Murmuring stream.

MAKINO: *ma:* stream; *kino:* bad.

MAKIRIKIRI: *ma:* stream; *kirikiri:* gravelly. Gravelly stream.

MAKOHINE: *ma:* stream; *kohine:* girl. Girls' stream.

MAKOTUKU: *ma:* stream; *kotuku:* white heron. Stream of the white heron. Alternatively, *kotuku* should be *kotukutuku:* fuchsia.

MAKOURA: *ma:* stream; *koura:* fresh-water crayfish ("crawlies"). Crayfish stream.

MAKOWHAI: *ma:* stream; *kowhai:* native tree. Kowhai stream. A name given by a Pakeha.

MAKU: wet.

MAKURI: *ma:* stream; *kuri:* dog. Dog creek.

Kowhai: native tree

MAMAKU : tree-fern.

MANA : power. Mana Island near Wellington is, in full, Te Mana - o - Kupe - ki - Aotea-roa, the ability of Kupe to cross the ocean to Aotearoa. It was Kupe's daughter who suggested that the name should be given to the island.

MANAIA : a carved Maori figure with beak. Manaia in Taranaki was named after a local Maori chief. Manaia, on the south side of Whangarei Harbour was named after a chief who climbed the hill. When at the summit he quarrelled with his wife and kicked her and his slave, and the whole family were turned into stones by the gods.

MANAKAU : *mana:* authority or prestige; *kau:* alone. Prestige alone. Te Rauparaha subdued the local inhabitants by means of his prestige without having to resort to war.

MANAPOURI : Short for manawa-popore. *Manawa:* heart; *popore:* throbbing. Anxious heart, a name given by a traveller whose canoe who was threatened by a storm. The true name of the lake is Moturau, meaning Many islands.

MANAROA: *mana:* power; *roa:* long.

MANAWAORA : *manawa:* heart; *ora:* healthy.

MANAWARU: anxious, apprehensive, or enraptured.

MANAWA-TAHI : out of breath. The name of the Three Kings Islands. The chief Raura owned one of them and swam across from the mainland, arriving exhausted on the shore of the island.

MANAWATU: heart standing still with fear, or depressed spirit. Haunui was pursuing his wife, and when he came to the river he held his hand to his heart and gave the name Manawatu, which means Heart stood still, or similar meanings.

MANGA - A - TE - TIPUA : *manga:* stream; *a:* of; *te:* the; *tipua:* demon. Goblin creek, a suitable name for the boiling stream at Ketetahi.

MANGAHAO : Short for Manga-a-hao. *manga:* stream; *a:* of; *hao:* netting. Stream where cockabullies are caught.

MANGAHARAKEKE: *manga:* stream; *harakeke:* flax. Flax creek.

MANGAHOE : *manga:* stream; *hoe:* to paddle. Paddling in the stream.

MANGAHUIA : *manga:* stream; *huia:* extinct bird. Huia stream.

MANGAITI : *manga:* stream; *iti:* small. Little stream.

MANGAKAHIA : *manga:* stream; *kahia* (or *kohia*) : passion vine. Passion vine stream.

MANGAKAIWHIRIA: *manga:* stream; *kaiwhiria:* climbing plant.

MANGAKINO: *manga:* stream; *kino:* bad. Useless stream.

MANGAKURA: *manga:* stream; *kura:* red, or red ochre. Red stream.

MANGAMAHOE: *manga:* stream; *mahoe:* whitewood tree. Mahoe stream.

MANGAMAHU: *manga:* stream; *mahu:* gentle. Gently flowing stream.

MANGAMAIRE: *manga:* stream; *maire:* tree (New Zealand olive). Maire stream.

MANGAMAKO: Probably short for Mangamakomako. *manga:* stream; *makomako:* wineberry tree. Wineberry stream.

Nikau: New Zealand palm

MANGAMATE: *manga:* stream; *mate:* death. Stream of death.

MANGAMAUNU: *manga:* barracouta fish; *maunu:* bait. Barracouta bait.

MANGAMINGI: Probably Mangamingimingi in full. *manga:* stream; *mingimingi:* shrub. Mingimingi stream.

MANGAMUKA: *manga:* stream; *muka:* shoot of *nikau.* Nikau palm stream.

MANGAMUTU: *manga:* stream; *mutu:* finished. Dead-end stream.

MANGANGARARA: *manga:* stream; *ngarara:* lizard. Lizard stream.

MANGANGUKAIOTA: I will eat you raw. Said by one chief to another if he dared to cross a line between them. The chief did so, and was eaten raw. *Manga:* scraps; *ngu:* eat greedily; *kai:* food; *ota:* raw.

MANGANUI: *manga:* stream; *nui:* big. Big stream.

MANGANUIATEAO: *manga:* stream; *nui:* big; *a:* of; *te:* the; *ao:* world. The great stream of the land. It is famous in legend, and has two other names equally pretentious: The powerful and famous river of Rongomai, and The river of ever-dancing waters and steep, echoing cliffs.

MANGAOHAE: the stream of Hae.

MANGAOHUTU: the stream of Hutu.

MANGAONE: *manga:* stream; *one:* beach. Sandy stream.

MANGAONOHO: *manga:* stream; *o:* of; *Noho:* proper name. Noho's stream.

MANGAORANGA: Correct name is Manga-o-Rongomai. *Manga:* stream; *o:* of; *Rongomai:* a god. Stream of Rongomai.

MANGAOTAKI: *manga:* stream; *o:* of; *Taki:* proper name. Taki's stream.

MANGAOWERA: *manga:* stream; *o:* of; *Wera:* proper name. Wera's stream.

MANGAPAI: *manga:* stream; *pai:* good. Stream of good water.

MANGAPAKEHA: The correct name is. Mangapakia. *manga:* stream; *pakia:* to be touched.

MANGAPAKIHI: *manga:* stream; *pakihi:* open grass country. Grassy stream.

MANGAPAPA: *manga:* stream; *papa:* flat country. Stream through the flat.

MANGAPEHI: *manga:* stream; *pehi:* sticks for making fire, or trouble. Stream of trouble.

MANGAPIKO: *manga:*

stream; *piko:* bent. Crooked stream.

MANGAPIRI: *manga:* stream; *piri:* to hide, or native burr. Hidden stream.

MANGAPOURI: *manga:* stream; *pouri:* dark. Dark stream.

MANGAPUAKA: *manga:* stream; *puaka:* bird-snare. Stream of the bird-snare.

MANGAPURUA: *manga:* stream; *purua:* abundant, or plenty. Stream of plenty.

MANGARAKAU: *manga:* stream; *rakau:* tree or timber. Stream by the trees.

MANGARAMARAMA: *manga:* stream; *ramarama:* myrtle tree.

MANGARATA: *manga:* stream; *rata:* tree. Rata stream.

MANGARAWA: *manga:* stream; *rawa:* swamp. Swampy stream.

MANGARENGARENGA: *manga:* stream; *rengarenga:* renga-lily. Stream of lilies.

MANGAREPOREPO: *manga:* stream; *reporepo:* soft mud. Muddy creek.

MANGARIMU: *manga:* stream; *rimu:* tree. Rimu stream.

MANGAROA: *manga:* stream; *roa:* long. Long stream.

MANGAROHUTU: *manga:* stream; *rohutu:* myrtle. Myrtle stream.

MANGARUA: *manga:* stream; *rua:* two. Two streams.

MANGATAINOKA: *manga:* stream; *tainoka:* native broom. Broom stream.

MANGATANGI: *manga:* stream; *tangi:* weeping. Babbling brook.

MANGATAPU: *manga:* stream; *tapu:* sacred. Forbidden stream.

MANGATARATA: *manga:* stream; *tarata:* tree. Tarata stream.

MANGATAWHIRI: *manga:* stream; *tawhiri:* tree. Stream where the tawhiri grows.

MANGATEA: *manga:* stream; *tea:* clear, or white. Clear stream.

MANGATERA: *manga:* stream; *te:* the; *ra:* sun. Sunny stream.

MANGATERE: *manga:* stream; *tere:* to flow. Flowing stream.

MANGATERETERE: *manga:* stream; *teretere:* swiftly flowing. Swift flowing stream.

MANGATINA: *manga:* stream; *tina:* exhausted. The first Maoris to reach the stream were exhausted by the effort of crossing.

MANGATINI: *manga:* stream; *tini:* many. Stream with many branches. The country this stream in the

Buller district flows through is very broken.

MANGATITI: *manga:* stream; *titi:* mutton bird. Stream of the mutton birds.

MANGATOETOE: *manga:* stream; *toetoe:* plume grass. Toetoe stream.

MANGATOKI: Possibly a contraction of Mangatitoki: *manga:* stream; *titoki:* tree. Titoki stream.

MANGATU: *ma:* stream; *ngatu:* part of the *raupo.* Stream of the reeds.

MANGAWAI: *manga:* stream; *wai:* water.

MANGAWARA: *manga:* stream; *wara:* indistinct sound.

MANGAWEKA: *manga:* stream; *weka:* wood-hen. Creek of the wood-hens.

MANGAWHAI: *manga:*

Weka: woodhen

stream; *Whai:* name of a chief. Te Whai fled from the Nga-Puhi and settled on the headland where the rivers meet. The name means River of Te Whai.

MANGAWHARARIKI: *manga:* stream; *wharariki:* a kind of flax. Stream where the flax grows.

MANGAWHARAWHARA: *manga:* stream. *wharawhara:* perching lily. Wharawhara stream.

MANGAWHARE: *manga:* stream; *whare:* house. Stream by the house.

MANGAWHATA: *manga:* stream; *whata:* raised storehouse. Stream by the storehouse.

MANGAWHERO: *manga:* stream; *whero:* red. Red stream.

MANGERE: lazy. When Ihenga crossed the Waikato, he came to this place and rested while his young men prepared food. They took so long that he was angry, and named the place Laziness.

MANGONUI: *mango:* shark; *nui:* big. Large shark.

MANGOPARERUA: two hammerhead sharks.

MANGOREI: *mango:* shark; *rei:* tooth. Shark's tooth.

MANGUNGU: closely knit, or woven.

MANIATOTO: The name in full is Maniaototo. *mania:* plain; *o:* of; *toto:* blood. It was the scene of many bloody battles.

MANIATUTU: *mania:* plain; *tutu:* tree. Plain where the tutu grows.

MANUHEREKIA: *manu:* bird; *herekia:* tied. The tied bird. A Maori scout tied a wounded *kaka* there to mark the crossing place.

MANUKA: tea-tree.

MANUKAU: *manu:* bird; *kau:* to wade. Wading birds. The original name of the Manukau Harbour was Manuka (tea-tree). It may have received this name when Kahu-mata-momoe set up a *manuka* post there as a *rahui* or sacred mark. On the other hand, it is likely that the name is of even greater antiquity. There is an old proverb which says, Kei te tua o Manuka, te kite muri ki te kupenga-o-Taramainuku (When you pass out beyond the Manuka waters, do not look back until you reach, or pass, the fishing net of Tara).

MANUNUI: Properly Mananui. *mana:* prestige; *nui:* large. Great prestige. It refers to the power and prestige of the chief Paparangi.

MANUPIRUA: two little birds.

MANUREWA: *manu:* kite; *rewa:* floating. Floating kite. A kite once broke loose at Onehunga and floated over Manurewa.

MANUTAHI: *manu:* bird; *tahi:* single. Solitary bird.

MANUTITI: *manu:* bird; *titi:* mutton-bird. The small island in Dusky Sound was so named because there was a colony of birds there, and the Maoris could always collect a few in the autumn.

MANUTUKE: *manu:* bird; *tuke:* elbow, or to twitch.

MANUWHAEA: *manu:* bird; *whaea:* split. The split bird.

MAORI: native to the country. When the word Maori enters into a name, as in Maori Hill, Maori Creek, etc., it is safe to say that it has been conferred by a Pakeha.

MAPERE: to fly.

MAPIU: In full, Mapiupui. *ma:* stream; *piupiu:* fern. Ferny creek.

MAPOU: native tree.

MAPOURIKA: The word is unknown. It may possibly be a South Island form of Mapouriki, q.v.

MAPOURIKI: *mapou:* tree; *riki:* little. The small mapou trees.

MAPUA: bearing abundance of fruit.

Marae: meeting ground

MARAEKAKAHO: *marae;* village assembly ground; *kakaho:* plumes of the *toetoe.* The courtyard surrounded by plume grass.

MARAEKURA: *marae:* courtyard; *kura:* man of prowess. When Turi reached the Kaupoko-nui River his enchanted cloak opened twice and spread out, and he called the place Maraekura.

MARAEROA: *marae:* courtyard; *roa:* long. Long plaza.

MARAETAI: *marae:* open space; *tai:* coast. Open space by the seashore.

MARAETUI: *marae:* open space; *tui:* sea. Flat area at the head of the bay.

MARAEWEKA: *marae:* courtyard; *weka:* woodhen. Weka on the marae.

MARAHAU: *mara:* garden; *hau:* wind. Windy garden.

MARAKEKE : Probably Marakerake, bald.

MARAMA : moon.

MARAMARUA : *marama:* month; *rua:* two. Two months.

MARANGAI : east wind.

MARANUI : The name in full should be Maraenui. *marae:* expanse; *nui:* big. Great expanse. It refers to the expanse of ocean visible from Lyall Bay.

MARAROA : *mara:* cultivation; *roa:* long. Long cultivated area.

MARARUA : *mara:* cultivation; *rua:* two. Two plantations.

MARAWHIUPUNGA-REHU : *mara:* cultivation; *whiu:* to throw; *pungarehu:* ashes. The cultivation overcast with ashes.

MARERETU : *marere:* to let down; *retu:* part of a fishing net. To let down the net. The original name has been contracted.

MAREWA : raised up, or light soil.

MARINO : calm, or peaceful.

MARIRI : unripe fruit of the tawa tree.

MAROKOPA : *maro:* kilt. or stiff; *kopa:* to fold, or lame. The place where Turi of the Aotea canoe folded his girdle, or where he went lame.

MAROMAKU : *maro:* girdle; *maku:* wet. Wet kilt.

MAROPIU : *maro:* kilt; *piu:* to swing. Kilt waving in the breeze.

MAROTIRI: *maro:* apron; *tiri:* to throw or place beside. Placed beside the apron.

MARUA : valley.

MARUAKOA : *marua:* valley; *koa:* glad. Happy valley.

MARUIA : sheltered, like a valley deep in the hills.

MATA : quartz, flint, or face.

MATAHARA : *mata:* surface; *hara:* ugly. Ugly surface.

MATAHIWI : *mata:* face; *hiwi:* ridge. The ridge above the cliff.

MATAHORUA : *mata:* face, or eye; *horua:* sobbing. Weeping.

MATAI : sea, or a native tree.

MATAIHUKA: black pine.

MATAINUI : *matai:* black pine; *nui:* big, or many. Plenty of black pine.

MATAIRANGI : an observation post on a hill, so named because of its commanding position on Tinakori Hill.

MATAITAKIARA: *matai:* look-out point; *takiara:*

morning star. The look-out point from which the morning star can be seen.

MATAIWHETU : *matai:* to look at; *whetu:* star. To gaze at the stars.

MATAKANA : distrustful, or wary.

MATAKANUI : *mata:* face; *ka:* blow, or scar; *nui:* big. The scarred face of a big cliff.

MATAKINOKINO: *mata:* face; *kinokino:* ugly. Ill-favoured face.

MATAKITAKI : to gaze at. The name was given to a number of places which Kupe and others inspected when they first came to New Zealand.

MATAKOHE: *mata:* headland; *kohe* (short for *kohekohe*) : a tree. Pinnacle of land where kohekohe trees grow.

MATAMATA : point, or extremity. The point of land on which the pa (fortified village) was built projected like a tongue into the surrounding swamp.

MATAMAU : stingy. Or *mata:* heap; *mau:* products of the soil. Heap of vegetables.

MATANEHUNEHU : *mata:* headland; *nehunehu:* spray. A headland drenched with flying spray. In a stiff northerly the spray flies right over the cliff.

MATANGI : breeze.

MATANGIRAU : *matangi:* breeze; *rau:* leaf. Wind among the leaves.

MATANUKU : *mata:* cliff; *nuku:* to move or extend. Kahumata-momoe came to a cliff where there was a stone projecting from the face, and he named it for this reason.

MATAPEHI - O - TE - RANGI : the first streak of dawn from the heavens. Maori name for McLaren's Peak, Nelson.

MATAPIA : *mata:* headland; *pia:* to bathe with water. Headland washed by the sea.

MATAPOURI : gloomy, a black teal or a shellfish.

MATAPU : to make clear of tapu. There was a prolific miro tree at this place which attracted flocks of pigeons. An old chief made it *tapu* or sacred to himself so that all the pigeons would be his. No doubt it became necessary to clear the tree of *tapu* at a later date if others were to have a share of the pigeons.

MATARAE : a headland.

MATARAU : a number of points, used in describing a rocky shore.

MATARAWA : *mata:* headland; *rawa:* numerous. Many headlands.

MATARIKI : the Pleiades,

or the north-east sea-breeze.

MATAROA : *mata:* headland; *roa:* long. Long headland.

MATATA : dividing waters.

MATATAPU : *mata:* headland; *tapu:* sacred. Sacred headland.

MATATOKI : *mata:* flint; *toki:* adze. Flint adze.

MATAU : fish-hook. At one place given to a river which has a bend resembling a fishhook, to another where there is a beach of the same shape. Matau, the original name for the Clutha River, was properly Mata-au, a current or eddy in an expanse of water.

MATAUIRA : *Mata:* point of land; *uira:* lightning, or gleaming.

MATAURA : reddish, eddy-

Matuku: bittern

ing water. The swamp water which drains into the river is impregnated with oxide of iron.

MATAURI : *ma:* stream; *tauri:* ornament of feathers.

MATAWAI: fountain head, or source of a spring.

MATAWHAURA: warfare.

MATAWHERO : *mata:* face; *whero:* red. Red face.

MATIAHA : after Matiaha Tira Morehu.

MATIERE : *ma:* stream; *tiere:* scent. Scented stream.

MATIU : Somes Island in Wellington Harbour was named after Matiu, the daughter of Kupe.

MATUKITUKI : *ma:*

Matau: fish-hook

stream; *tukituki:* dashing. The dashing or pounding stream. The Matukituki River was probably named after a chief.

MATUKU : bittern, or blue heron.

MAUKU : small ground ferns.

MAUNGAATUA: *maunga:* mountain; *atua:* god. Mountain of the gods.

MAUNGAHARURU : *maunga:* mountain; *haruru:* rumbling. Rumbling mountain. When the Takitimu canoe was travelling down the east coast on its way to search for greenstone, a high inland range was seen. The *tohunga* (priest) took a piece of wood which received life and flew to the top of the range in the shape of a bird. The mountain gave forth a rumbling sound.

MAUNGAHAUMI : *maunga:* mountain; *haumi:* piece of wood used to lengthen a canoe. When at Whakatane, Pawa the captain sent a party of men ashore to get a suitable piece of timber for a topside plank for the canoe, and they found it at this mountain.

MAUNGAHUKA:*maunga:* mountain; *huka:* snow. Snowy mountain. This peak in the Tararuas was usually snow-covered.

MAUNGAHURA: *maunga:* mountain; *hura:* bare. Bald mountain.

MAUNGAKARAMEA: *maunga:* mountain; *karamea:* red ochre. There are many colours in the mountain, which is known to the Pakeha as Rainbow Mountain.

MAUNGAKIEKIE : *maunga:* mountain; *kiekie:* plant. The mountain where the kiekie grows abundantly. It is the Maori name for One Tree Hill in Auckland.

MAUNGANAMU : *maunga:* mountain; *namu:* sandfly. Sandfly mountain.

MAUNGANUI : *maunga:* mountain; *nui:* big. Large mountain.

MAUNGAPOHATU : *maunga:* mountain; *pohatu:* rock. Rocky mountain.

MAUNGARAKI: *maunga:* mountain; *raki:* north. Mountains running in a northerly direction.

MAUNGA TANIWHA : *maunga:* mountain; *taniwha:* monster. Taniwha mountain. Maori name for Mount Camel.

MAUNGATAPERE : *maunga:* mountain; *tapere:* place for meeting. Meeting place of mountains.

MAUNGATAPU: *maunga:* mountain; *tapu:* sacred or forbidden. Forbidden mountain.

MAUNGATAUTARI :

maunga: mountain; *tautari:* upright stick. Maungatautari was the ancient name for Cambridge.

MAUNGATI : *maunga:* mountain; *ti:* cabbage-tree. Cabbage-tree mountain.

MAUNGATIKI : *maunga:* mountain; *tiki:* fungus. Mountain where the fungus grows.

MAUNGATUA : Properly Maungaatua. *maunga:* mountain; *atua:* god or spirit. Mountain of the spirits.

MAUNGATUROTO : *maunga:* mountain; *tu:* to stand; *roto:* lake. Mountain standing in a lake. Several of the volcanic peaks in North Auckland are surrounded by swamps, which were originally lagoons.

MAUNGAWERA: *maunga:* mountain; *wera:* hot, or burnt. Burnt mountain.

MAUNGAWHAU : *maunga:* mountain; *whau:* native tree. Whau hill.

MA-WARO : *ma:* stream; *waro:* charcoal. Charcoal stream.

MAWHERA : widespread river mouth. It refers to the broad mouth of the Grey River, and is the site of Greymouth.

MAWHERAITI : little Mawhera, a tributary of the Mawhera of Grey River.

MEREMERE: evening star.

MERETOTO: *mere:* green-

Mere: greenstone club

stone club; *toto:* blood. Blood-drinking club. It is the Maori name for Ship Cove.

MIHAMIHANUI : *mihamiha:* to begin to grow; *nui:* large. A large patch of growing vegetation.

MIHIWAKA : *mihi:* to greet; *waka:* canoe. To greet the canoe. It is said that when the Mihiwaka tunnel was being constructed, a store was kept by Mrs. Walker. The Maori labourers gave the Maori pronunciation to her name, and Mrs. Walker became Mihiwaka.

MIKI : a ridge of hills. Named after a woman who was carried away by the *maeroero* or wild men.

MIKIMIKI : surprised expression. It is said that the full

name is Mimikitanga - o - te - mata-o-Ngatuere. The Wairarapa was being invaded by a force of Hauhaus and were met unexpectedly by the chief Ngatuere Tawhirimatea Tawhao, who had a surprised look on his face when he saw them. This is the meaning of the long name, The surprised look on the face of Ngatuere.

MIKO : young shoot of the nikau palm.

MIMI : stream, or creek.

MIMIHAU : passing shower.

MINA : to desire.

MINARAPA : *mina:* to desire; *rapa:* to seek for. To look for something earnestly desired. The stream on Mount Egmont was named after Minarapa who accompanied Bell and Carrington when they climbed the mountain.

MIROWHARERA : *miro:* native tree; *whare:* house; *ra:* The miro tree which shades the house from the sun. The name appears on early maps as Merofafara, and is suggested that it was a Maori attempt to pronounce Meadowbank, as there was gum-diggers' settlement of that name in the locality at Waipoua Forest.

MITIMITI : shallow water.

MITITAI: *miti:* to lap; *tai:* the coast. To lap the coast.

Insects flew so close to the water here that they seemed to lick it.

MOA : large, extinct, flightless bird. Most places such as Moa Flat, Moa Creek, Moa Point, etc. have been so named because of the large number of moa bones found in the vicinity.

MOANA : ocean, or large lake.

MOANA - KOTUKU : *moana:* large lake; *kotuku:* white heron. Lake of the white heron. Maori name for Lake Brunner where the *kotuku* would often be seen.

MOANA - NUI - A - KIWA : *moana:* ocean; *nui:* big; *a:* of; *Kiwa:* a god. The great ocean of Kiwa. The Pacific Ocean.

MOANATAIARI : *moana:* ocean; *taiari:* dashing. The stormy ocean.

MOANAWHENUA - POURI : *moana:* ocean; *whenua:* land; *pouri:* sad, or dark. Sombre sound, the Maori name for Edwardson Arm in Fiordland, notable because there was usually a cloud over it casting a dark shadow.

MOAWHANGO : *moa:* large extinct bird; *whango:* hoarse. Wheezy moa. *Whango* may be a corruption of *whanga,* valley, thus giving Moa valley.

MOEAWATEA : *moe:* to

sleep; *awatea:* daylight. Sleeping in the daytime.

MOEHAU : *moe:* to sleep; *hau:* wind. Windy sleeping place. The name in full is Moehau-o-Tama-te-kapua. Tama-te-kapua, captain of the Arawa canoe was buried at Cape Colville, and the name was given by his son Kahu-mata-momoe. *Hau* probably refers to the life-essence, and the name means The sleeping sacredness of Tama-te-kapua. It may also mean The wind resting, or sleeping.

MOENGAWAHINE : *mo-enga:* bed; *wahine:* woman. Woman's bed.

MOERA: *moe:* to sleep; *ra:* the sun. Sleeping in the sun.

MOERAKI : *moe:* to sleep; *raki* (South Island form of *rangi*) : sky, or day. A place for sleep by day.

MOERANGI : *moe:* to

Haka: war dance

sleep; *rangi:* sky. Sleepy sky.

MOEREWA: *moe:* to sleep; *rewa:* floating like a bird apparently asleep. To sleep on high.

MOEROA : *moe:* to sleep; *roa:* long. Long sleep, or resting, or sleeping place.

MOETAPU : *moe:* to sleep; *tapu:* sacred. Sacred sleep.

MOETERE : *moe:* to sleep; *tere:* swift. Swift sleep. Named after Moetere who died in a snowstorm here on the Huiarau Range.

MOHAKA : *mo:* used for; *haka:* dance. Place used for a dance. The name was imported from Hawaiki.

MOHAKATINO : *mo:* used; *haka:* dance; *tino:* exact, precise. The river was named because Turi of the Aotea canoe departed in person *(tino)* after having slept at Mokau.

MOIOIO: the little blue penguin.

MOKAI : captive.

MOKAU : sleeping place. Named by Turi because he slept there.

MOKAUITI : little Mokau.

MOKIHINUI : *mokihi:* raft of dry flax stalks; *nui:* big. Large raft.

MOKO HINAU : *moko:* lizard; *hinau:* native tree.

MOKOIA : tattooed. On Mokoia Island, Lake Rotorua,

61

a chief was fatally stabbed over the eye in a closely tattooed place with a sharpened *ko* (digging implement), and the name is a pun : *moko:* tattoo; *ko:* digging implement. On the other hand, Mokoia, which was the original name for Panmure, was Mokoika, named after the *taniwha* (water monster) Mokoikahikuwaru, the lizard with eight tails.

MOMONA : good, fertile land.

MOMORANGI : *momo:* offspring; *rangi:* the sky. Offspring of heaven.

MONOWAI : The proper name is Manokiwai; *mano:* a fixed channel; *ki:* full; *wai:* water. Channel full of water. It is a long narrow lake which is always full, although it receives no big streams or rivers. Monowai was as close as James McKerrow, the Pakeha discoverer, could get to the Maori name.

MORERE : a swing, or "giant stride".

MORORIMU : *moro:* wave; *rimu:* bull kelp. Kelp floating on the waves. A Maori chief who raided the pa reported his success by saying, "Nothing now moves at Waipapa but the kelp in the sea."

MOTATAU : Properly Motautau, talking to oneself. In this place Ihenga was heard talking to himself.

MOTITI : named after a place in Hawaiki because there was no firewood there. There is a proverb which concerns the Arawa canoe : Kei Motiti koe e noho ana : I suppose you are at Motiti, as you can find no firewood. Lit. extirpated.

MOTU : island, or isolated clump of trees.

MOTUARA : *motu:* island; *ara:* path. Island in the path of the canoe.

MOTU-AROHIA : *motu:* island; *arohia:* reconnoitred. The island that was spied upon.

MOTUEKA: In full, Motu-weka. *motu:* clump of trees;

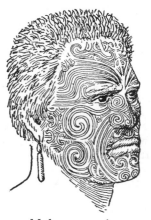

Moko: tattooing

weka: wood-hen. Wood-hens in a grove of trees. The name originally came from Hawaiki, where it may have a different connotation. It is sometimes said to mean The crippled wood-hen—one which was kept as a lure to capture wekas.

MOTUHORA : whale island. This is the name given to it by the Pakeha. In that case it should be Motutohora. It could also mean *motu:* clumps of trees; *hora:* scattered. Scattered patches of bush.

MOTUIHE : *motu:* island; *Ihe:* short for Ihenga. The island was named after his nephew Ihenga by Kahu-mata-momoe.

MOTUKANAE : *motu:* island; *kanae:* mullet. Mullet island.

MOTUKARAKA : *motu:* island; *karaka:* native tree. Island of the karaka trees.

MOTUKARARA : *motu:* island; *karara* (South Island form of *ngarara*) : lizard. Lizard island.

MOTUKAUATIITI : *motu:* grove of trees; *kauati:* rubbing sticks to make fire; *iti:* little. Little fire-making tree grove. This was Corsair Bay, and Motukauatirahi (*rahi* meaning large) was Cass Bay. Both bays were noted for their groves of kaikomako trees, the timber of which is specially suitable for fire-making.

MOTUKAUATIRAHI : See under Motukauatiiti.

MOTUKAURI : *motu:* island; *kauri:* native tree. Kauri island. The small island in the Hokianga River was covered with kauris.

MOTUKIEKIE : *motu:* island; *kiekie:* plant. This is the Maori name for Stop Island in Dusky Sound. It is one of the few places in the sound where the *kiekie* grows.

MOTUKINA : *motu:* island; *kina:* sea-egg. The island of sea-eggs.

MOTUKIORE : *motu:* island; *kiore:* rat. Rat island. The island at the mouth of the Motueka River was infested by

Karaka: New Zealand tree

rats, and had to be abandoned for cultivation purposes.

MOTUNAU : *motu:* island. *nau:* scurvy grass. The grass grew here until it was eaten off by cattle.

MOTUNGARARA : *motu:* island; *ngarara:* lizard. Lizard island.

MOTUNUI : *motu:* island; *nui:* big. Big island.

MOTUPIKO: *motu:* clump of trees; *piko:* winding, or curved. Straggling clumps of trees.

MOTUPIPI : *motu:* island; *pipi:* shellfish. Pipi island.

MOTUPIU : *motu:* island; *piu:* to swing. Swinging island. This is Dog Island near Bluff. The story is that a southern tribe found a huge piece of greenstone in the sea. They drove it round to Bluff by following it in three canoes. It nearly eluded them several times and finally came to rest, where it remained as an island.

MOTUPOUA : *motu:* island; *poua:* old man. Old man island. An old chief was buried on the summit of the hill.

MOTURATA : *motu:* island; *rata:* native tree. Rata island. Whale Island at Taieri Mouth and other places of this name were often bright with the scarlet blossoms of the rata.

MOTURAU : *motu:* island; *rau:* many, or a hundred. A hundred islands. The proper name for Lake Manapouri, q.v.

MOTUROA : *motu:* island; *roa:* long, or tall. Long island. There are many places with this name. Moturoa is the largest of the islands in the Bay of Islands, whereas Muturoa in Queen Charlotte Sound is small, and there probably means Tall island.

MOTURUA: *motu:* island; *rua:* two, or a pit. Two islands, Island with a pit.

MOTUTAIKO : *motu:* island; *taiko:* mutton - bird. Mutton-bird island.

MOTUTAPU : *motu:* island; *tapu:* sacred, or forbidden. Forbidden island.

MOTUTARA : *motu:* island; *tara:* gull. Gull island. Motutara Island in Lake Rotorua is frequented by the *tarapunga,* the little lake gull.

MOTUTAWA : *motu:* island; *tawa:* native tree. Tawa island.

MOTU-TAWAKI : *motu:* island; *tawaki:* big, or crested penguin. Penguin island. Maori name for Passage Island.

MOTUTERE : *motu:* island; *tere:* floating. Floating island. The name is found in several places; among others it is the Maori name for Castle Rock at Coromandel, which looks like an island floating in the sky when it is surrounded by mist.

MOTUTIEKE: *motu:* island; *tieke:* saddleback bird. Saddleback island.

MOUREA: remnant. A name which comes from the Society Group.

MOUTAPU: *mou:* fixed; *tapu:* sacred. On this island in the Grey River the Maoris placed the bones of their dead in the branches of *kahikatea,* thus making them *tapu.*

MOUTERE: island.

MOUTUA: In full. Motu-toa. *motu:* island; *toa:* warrior. An island where warriors fought. ·

MOUTOHORA: See Motuhora.

MURI-AROHA-O-KAHU: *muri:* breeze; *aroha:* affection; *o:* of; *Kahu:* Kahu-mata-mo-moe. Kahu-mata-momoe came to a dividing of the river Waihou and rested. As he felt the soft breeze, words of affection came to his lips.

MURIHIKU: *muri:* end; *hiku:* tail. End of the tail. So named because it is the southern end of the South Island.

MURITAI: *muri:* breeze; *tai:* tide. Sea-breeze.

MURIWAI: *muri:* end; *wai:* water. Backwater or the junction of streams.

MURIWHENUA: *muri:* end; *whenua:* land. End of the land. Land's end. Maori name for North Cape.

MURUPARA: *muru:* to wipe off; *para:* mud. To wipe off the mud.

N

NAENAE: sandfly.

NAMU: sandfly.

NAUMAI: Come!

NEHUTAI: sea-spray.

NGAERE: swamp.

NGAHAPE: *nga:* the; *hape:* hunchback, or cripple. The cripples.

NGAHERE: the forest.

NGAHINEPOURI: *nga:*

Nga hine: the women

the; *hine:* women; *pouri:* sad. The sorrowing women.

NGAIO : a native tree.

NGAIONUI : *ngaio:* native tree; *nui:* big. The big ngaio.

NGA - KARIKARI - A - RAKAIHAUTU : *nga:* the; *karikari:* excavations; *a:* of; *Rakaihautu:* South Island giant. The diggings of Rakaihautu. The great series of cold lakes in the South Island which were supposed to have been dug by Rakaihautu.

NGAKAWAU : the shags.

NGA-KURI-HINE-POU-POU : *nga:* the; *kuri:* dog; *hine:* girl; *poupou:* plunged in. The dogs of the girl who plunged in.

NGAKUTA: edible seaweed which was found at these bays.

NGA - MAKAWE - O - MAAHU : *nga:* the; *makawe:* hair; *o:* of; *Maahu:* a chief who engaged the rainbow god in conflict. The hairs of Maahu. They are represented by the flax which grows on the cliff.

NGAMATAPOURI : *nga:* the; *matapouri:* black teal.

NGAMOANA : *nga:* the; *moana:* pit-covers.

NGAMOKO : *nga:* the; *moko:* lizards.

NGAMOTU : *nga:* the; *motu:* islands.

NGAONE : *nga:* the; *one:* sands.

NGAPAENGA : *nga:* the; *paenga:* boundaries.

NGA PAKIHI - WHAKA - TEKATEKA-A-WAITAHA : *nga:* the; *pakihi:* open plains; *whakatekateka:* to strut; *a:* of; *Waitaha:* South Island tribe. The plain where the Waitaha people gave vent to their joyful feeling in playful exuberance. This was the old name for the Canterbury Plains when they were first discovered.

NGAPARA : The name should really be Ngatepara. *nga:* the; *tepara:* tables. It is a Pakeha invention, the equivalent of table-lands.

NGAPOHATU : *nga:* the; *pohatu:* rocks. The rocks.

NGA POITU - O - TE - KUPENGA-A-TARAMA-INUKU : the floats of the net of Taramainuku. These are the islands of the Hauraki Gulf. See Te Kupenga-a-Tarama-inuku.

NGAPUHI: *nga:* the; *puhi:* plumes. The decorative plumes at the bow of a war canoe. Also the name of the North Auckland tribe.

NGAPUKE : *nga:* the; *puke:* hills.

NGAPUNA : *nga:* the; *puna:* springs.

NGAROMA : *nga:* the; *roma:* currents.

NGAROTO : *nga:* the; *roto:* lakes.

NGARUAWAHIA : *nga:* the; *rua:* pits; *wahia:* broken into. The plundered kumara pits. The local tribe was entertaining a large party of visitors, and the store-pits of kumaras (sweet potatoes) had to be broken into to provide sufficient food.

NGATAKI : *nga:* the; *taki:* flocks of whiteheads (birds).

NGATAMIRO: *ngata:* dry; *miro:* tree. Dry miro tree.

NGATAPA: *nga:* the; *tapa:* edges.

NGATIMOTI : belonging to Timothy. A Maori carved his name on a tree. The words were *na Timoti,* which means Belonging to Timothy, and were changed to Ngatimoti because it looked more like a Maori word.

NGATIRA : *nga:* the; *tira:* parties of travellers.

NGA TUAHU : *nga:* the; *tuahu:* sacred places.

NGA TUTU-MAHANGA-A-KAU-KOHEA : the twin tutu heads of Kau-kohea. When crossing the summit of a hill, a chief killed a hawk that was flying over with a sweep of his club. Not to be outdone the other, Kau-kohea, made a slash at two tutu bushes growing there, and gave the name.

NGAURANGA : *nga:* the; *uranga:* people who came by canoe.

NGAURUHOE : the name of a slave girl (Auruhoe) who was thrown into the crater to appease the gods. There are two literal translations. That Ngatoro-i-rangi threw his grandson Hoe into the crater. The plumes of smoke represent his hair. *nga:* the; *uru:* hairs; *Hoe:* Ngatoro's grandson. The hairs of Hoe. The other is *nga:* the; *uru:* the act of arranging hot stones in a *hangi* (oven); *hoe:* to toss out. When the mountain is in eruption it tosses out the hot stones.

NGAURUKEHU: *nga:* the; *urukehu:* fair-haired people. The place of this name in Nelson was The red hairs, because a chief likened the prolific growth of the flax to his own red hair.

NGAWAKA : *nga:* the; *waka:* canoes.

NGAWAPURUA : *nga:* the; *awa:* waters; *purua:* blocked up. The blocked up waters. An alternative, Nga-waipurua meaning The meeting of the waters, has been suggested.

NGAWARI : soft.

NGAWARO : *nga:* the; *waro:* burning coals.

NGAWHA : boiling springs.

Ngawha: hot springs

NGAWHAKAPAKOKO :
nga: the; *whakapakoko:* carved posts or palisades.

NGA WHATU : *nga:* the; *whatu:* eyes. When the Maoris passed these rocks in Cook Strait, they veiled the eyes of those who were passing them for the first time, as otherwise the voyagers would meet with disaster. Another version is that Kupe placed the eye-balls of the octopus he killed on The Brothers, which thus became a tapu or sacred place.

NGAWI : native grass.

NGONGOTAHA : *ngongo:* to drink; *taha:* calabash. To drink from a calabash. Ihenga ascended this mountain and met a fairy woman who gave him a drink from her calabash.

Then he was afraid and ran away, but gave the name to the river and mountain.

NGUNGURU : to sigh or to groan.

NGUTUNUI : *ngutu:* lip; *nui:* big. Big lip.

NGUTUWERA : *ngutu:* lip; *wera:* burnt. Burnt lips.

NIHOMANGA : *niho:* thorn; *manga:* stream. Thorny stream.

NIHONIHO : young shoots or buds.

NIHOTUPU : *niho:* tooth; *tupu:* broken. Decayed or broken teeth.

NIKAU : native palm.

NOKOMAI : a corruption of Nukumai. Move this way towards the person speaking.

NUHAKA : a place-name which comes from Hawaiki. There is no Maori equivalent.

NUKUHOU : *nuku:* to move; *hou:* feather. Moving feather.

NUKUNUKU : to move away.

NUKUROA : far-stretching land. An old name for the North Island.

O

OAKURA : the place of the flashing of the redness. Turi of the Aotea canoe had a red cloak which when spread out at this place was a symbol of his *mana* (prestige).

OAMARU : the place of the god Maru.

OAMURU : the place of the flesh left to dry. The flesh of conquered warriors was brought here to be preserved.

OAONUI : *o:* the place of; *ao:* cloud; *nui:* big. The place of a large cloud.

OARO : *o:* the place of; *aro:* bog. A boggy place.

OEO : *o:* the place of; *eo:* louse. The place of lice.

OHAEAWAI : the place of thermal water.

OHAI : *o:* the place of; *hai:* stone used in a game.

OHAKEA : *oha:* to repeat incantations over; *kea:* a lie; or false. Imperfect incantations.

OHAKUNE : *o:* the place of; *hakune:* to be careful. A place to be careful in. Hakune is probably a personal name.

OHARIU : The correct name is Owhariu. It means The place where Kupe turned aside to dry the sails of his canoe.

OHAU : The place of Hau, a noted traveller or name-giver. His full name was Haunui-a-Nania. Elsewhere the name means Windy place. Ohau Stream in Rotorua was the place of Ihenga's dog, Hau,

who was drowned in a whirl-pool.

OHAUPO : the place of Haupo. Or, *o:* the place of; *hau:* wind; *po:* night. The place of night winds.

OHAWE : *o:* the place of; *hawe:* bend in a river or road.

OHIA : to approve, or to think on the spur of the moment.

OHIKANUI : to perform rites with incantations. Two bands of warriors separated here, and one party was provided with food. The incantations were chanted to secure their return.

OHINEHOE : the place of Hinehoe. Literally, the place of an unpleasant girl.

OHINEKOPIRI : *o:* the place of; *hine:* girl; *kopiri:* The place of a young girl. Her name Punohu. She was assaulted, and her father died in her defence. Her body was hidden in a kumara pit, but was revealed by the presence of hawks, and she was avenged.

OHINEMUTU : *o:* the place of; *hine:* girl; *mutu:* cut off. The place of the young woman who was killed. Hine-te-kakara (the fragrant maid) was the daughter of Ihenga. After her death she was thrown into a boiling mud pool. To punish the murderers, Ihenga set up a memorial stone and called it Ohinemutu.

OHINEPANEA: the place of Hinepanea.

OHINERAU: the place of Hinerau. She was a female goddess of whirlwinds.

OHINEREHIA: the place of Hinerehia, who was a legendary mermaid.

OHINETAHI: the place of one daughter (daughter of Manuwhiri).

OHINEWAI: the place of Hinewai. Literally, The place of the water girl.

OHINGAHAPE: the place of the crooked foot. Named by Tiri after the crooked foot of Tua-nui-a-te-ra.

OHINGAITI: the place of Hingaiti. Literally *o:* of; *hinga:* childhood; *iti:* small, or unimportant.

OHIRO: *o:* the place of; *hiro:* dark, or stormy. A stormy place. The correct spelling is Owhiro, and it may commemorate Whiro, the explorer.

OHIWA: *o:* the place of; *hiwa:* watchful, or alert. The place of watching.

OHOKA: *o:* the place of; *hoka:* stake to which a decoy parrot is tied.

OHOTU: the place of Hotu. Literally, *o:* the place of; *hotu:* the fifteenth night of the moon.

OHOUKAKA: *o:* the place of; *hou-kaka:* parrot feather. The place of the parrot's feather. Ihenga took a feather from his hair and stuck it in the ground, and it became a *taniwha* (monster).

OHURA: the place of Hura. Literally, *o:* the place of; *hura:* to uncover.

OIHI: *o:* the place of; *ihi:* power, or authority.

OIO: *o:* the place of; *io:* a spur.

OKA: *o:* the place of; *ka:* to burn. The place of burning or cooking. This was Shelly Beach, Auckland. Great catches of fish were made in the Waitemata and the people camped on the beach and kept the cooking fires going.

OKAHAU: *oka:* knife; *hau:* famous. Famous knife.

OKAHUKURA: *o:* the place of; *kahu:* garment; *kura:* red. The place of the red garment. Kahukura was the god of the rainbow.

OKAIAWA: *o:* the place of; *kai:* food; *awa:* river. The place of food by the river, or in the valley.

OKAIHAU: *o:* the place of; *kaihau:* vagabond (literally, one who eats wind).

OKARAHIA: the place of calling in vain. Some fugitives were surprised and killed here.

OKARAMIO : Correctly, Okuramio, the place of the plume of the miromiro (tomtit).

OKAREKA : *o:* food for a journey; *kareka:* sweet. Tasty food for travellers.

OKARITO : *o:* the place of; *karito:* bulrush. A place where bulrushes grow plentifully.

OKATAINA : *o:* the place of; *kataina:* laughter. The place of laughing. The full name is Te Moana-i-kataina-e-Te-Rangitakaroro, The ocean laughed at by Te Rangitakaroro. It has been suggested humorously that Rangitakaroro may well have laughed at the thought of the tiny lake Okataina being described as an ocean.

OKATO: the place of Kato. Literally, The place of the tidal wave, or the full-flowing tide.

OKAU : *o:* the place of; *kau:* swimming or wading. The swimming place.

OKAUIA : the place of Kauia. Literally, The place of articles threaded on a stick.

OKERE : *o:* the place of; *kere:* to drift, or float.

OKETE-UPOKO : *o:* the place of; *kete:* basket; *upoko:* head. The place where baskets full of human heads were kept.

The famous warrior Te Rangiwhakaputa captured the locality of Lyttelton from the Ngati-Mamoe and kept the heads of the slain in baskets.

OKIATO : *o:* the place of; *kiato:* a receptacle for holding sacred objects.

OKIORE : *o:* the place of; *kiore:* rat.

OKIWI : *o:* the place of; *kiwi:* flightless bird. The place of the kiwi.

OKOKE : *o:* the place of; *koke:* moving forwards.

OKOKI : the place of the Koki canoe, which belonged to early inhabitants of New Zealand; *koki:* small canoe.

OKONGA : *o:* the place of; *konga:* running waters.

OKOROIRE : *o:* the place of; *koroire:* an extinct duck which once was plentiful here.

OKOWHIU : *oko:* wooden bowl; *whiu:* to throw, or place.

Kiwi: flightless bird

To place a wooden bowl. An Arai-te-uru name.

OKUI : *o:* the place of; *kui:* an underground insect. This is a very old name, because Kui was supposed to be one of the first people to live in New Zealand. He was an immediate descendant of Tuputupuwhenua, who was left in New Zealand by Maui.

OKUKU : *o:* the place of; *kuku:* shining cuckoo. The Pakeha called the place Cuckoo Hills and this was changed to "Maori" form, Okuku. *Kuku* is not the wood-pigeon, therefore, but the shining cuckoo.

OKUPE : *o:* the place of; *Kupe:* the famous explorer.

OKUPU : *o:* the place of; *kupu:* message.

OKURI : *o:* the place of; *kuri:* dog.

OKURU : *o:* the place of; *kuru:* weary. The place of weariness.

OMAHANUI : *o:* the place of; *maha:* pleasure; *nui:* great. The place of happiness.

OMAHU : the place of Mahu. Literally, The place of healing.

OMAHURI : *o:* the place of; *mahuri:* young trees.

OMAHUTA : *o:* the place of; *mahuta:* to rise. The place of rising, or landing from a canoe.

OMAIO : *o:* the place of; *maio:* calm. A calm spot.

OMAKA : *o:* the place of; *maka* (South Island form of *manga*) : stream.

OMAKAU : belonging to husband and wife, i.e. the baby. There are three rocks here, the father, mother, and the smallest, Omakau.

OMAMARI : the place of the Mamari canoe. This famous canoe, which came from Hawaiki, was wrecked at Maunganui Bluff, and is petrified as a group of rocks.

OMANAIA : *o:* the place of; *manaia:* carved figure with beak.

OMANAWA : *o:* the place of; *manawa:* mangrove.

OMANU : *o:* the place of; *manu:* birds.

OMAPERE : *o:* the place of; *mapere:* a species of *toetoe* (plume grass).

OMARAMA : the place of Marama. Literally, *o:* the place of; *marama:* moon, or light.

OMATA : *o:* the place of; *mata:* quartz.

OMAUI : *o:* the place of; *Maui:* the great explorer.

OMIHI : *o:* the place of; *mihi:* lamentations. The place of this name in Canterbury was originally Omimi.

OMIMI : *o:* the place of; *mimi:* a stream.

OMOANA : *o:* the place of; *moana:* the ocean.

OMOKOROA : the place of Mokoroa. Literally, *o:* the place of; *mokoroa:* a large white grub.

ONAEROA : *o:* the place of; *naeroa:* mosquito.

ONAMALUTU : Obviously an incorrect spelling. It is probably Onamahutu, the place of a cave, and it has been suggested that as the entrance to the valley is narrow, it has something of the appearance of a cave.

ONAWE : the place set on fire. Te Rauparaha set fire to this village on the Onawe Peninsula in Akaroa Harbour.

ONEHUNGA : *o:* the place of; *nehunga:* burial. There were burial places on the shore.

ONEKAKA : *one:* sand; *kaka:* hot. A descriptive name.

ONEKAKARA : *one:* beach; *kakara:* cockle shell, or smelly. Either Cockle shell beach, or Smelly beach. As the beach at Waikouaiti was part of a whaling station, it would certainly have had an evil smell.

ONEPOTO : *one:* beach; *poto:* short. Short, sandy beach.

ONEPU : *one:* sand; *pu:* loose. Loose sand.

ONEPUA : foam of the sea.

ONERAHI : *one:* beach; *rahi:* extensive. Long, sandy beach.

ONEROA : *one:* beach; *roa:* long. Long beach.

ONETAHUA : *one:* sand; *tahua:* heaped up. The name for Farewell Spit, and the sand dunes.

ONETAHUTI : *one:* sand; *tahuti:* to run along. Running along the beach.

ONETANGI : *one:* sand; *tangi:* sounding. The sounding sands.

ONETAPU : *one:* sand; *tapu:* sacred. Sacred sand.

ONETEA : *one:* sand; *tea:* white. White sand.

ONEWHERO : *one:* beach; *whero:* red. Red beach.

ONGAONGA : nettle.

ONGAROTO : *o:* the place of; *nga:* the; *roto:* lakes. The place of the lakes.

ONGARUE : *o:* the place of; *ngarue:* shaking, as in an earthquake.

ONIAO : *o:* the place of; *niao:* gunwale of a canoe.

ONOKE : *o:* the place of; *noke:* earthworm.

OPAHEKE : *o:* the place of; *paheke:* slip. The place where the slip occurred.

OPAKI : *o:* the place of; *paki:* fine weather.

OPAPA : *o:* the place of; *papa:* flat land.

OPARA : *o:* the place of;

para: mud. Muddy place.

OPARAE : *o:* the place of; *parae:* open country.

OPARAPARA : *o:* the place of; *parapara:* scum on the beach.

OPARARA: *o:* the place of; *parara:* to lie open towards. The shallow bay faces the Tasman Sea.

OPARAU : *o:* the place of; *pa:* fortified village; *rau:* many. The place of many fortified villages.

OPATU : *o:* the place of; *patu:* to strike. The place of striking.

OPAWA : The correct form of the name is Opaawaho, the place of the outer or seaward

Pa: fortified village

pa (village). This is the meaning of the name of Christchurch Opawa. The Opawa River in Marlborough is said to be Opaoa, smoky river, because the brown swamp water which poured into it gave it this appearance.

OPEPE : *o:* the place of; *pepe:* moth.

OPIHI : *o:* the place of; *pihi:* springing up, referring to plants. The place of good growth.

OPOHO : the place of Poho. Literally, *o:* the place of; *poho:* chest, or stomach.

OPONAE : *o:* the place of; *ponae:* a small basket.

OPONONI : the place of Pononi.

OPOTIKI : the place of Potiki. He was Potiki-mai-Tawhiti, Potiki from Tahiti. Literally, The place of children.

OPOURI : *o:* the place of; *pouri:* sadness.

OPOUTAMA : the place of Poutama. Literally, *o:* the place of; *poutama:* pattern on the reed walls of a house.

OPOUTERE : *o:* the place of; *pou:* post; *tere:* to float. The place of the floating post.

OPUA : the place of Pua. Literally, *o:* the place of; *pua:* flower.

OPUATIA : *o:* the place of; *pua:* flowers; *tia:* to stick in.

74

Poutama: reed pattern

The place of adorning with flowers.

OPUNAKE: the place of Punake. Literally, *o:* the place of; *punake:* bow of a canoe.

OPURA: *o:* the place of; *pura:* dust in the eye. The place where Tamatea got dust in his eye.

OPURERE: the place of flying mist.

ORAKAU: *o:* the place of; *rakau:* trees.

ORAKEI: *o:* the place of; *rakei:* adorning.

ORAKEI - KORAKO: *o:* the place of; *rakei:* adorning; *korako:* white sinter. This beautiful hot pool with its glowing colours was used as a place where chiefs attended to their toilet.

ORANA: Correctly Oranga: welfare.

ORANOA: escaping with difficulty.

ORAPIU: *ora:* alive, or escaped; *piu:* to throw.

ORARI: the place of Rari. Literally, *o:* the place of; *rari:* a fish.

ORATIA: *o:* the place of; *ra:* sun; *tia:* persistency. The place of the long-lingering sun.

ORAWAITE: When Reuben Waite, the first store-keeper on the West Coast, arrived with supplies for the gold-diggers, the Maoris called joyfully, "Ora, Waite !" This may be a contraction of "Kia ora, Waite !" Welcome Waite. See also Orowaiti.

OREPUKI: favourable weather; or, *aropi ki:* a cliff washed by high tides. A party of Maoris was once drowned there when trying to pass at high tide.

ORERE: *o:* the place of; *rere:* the waterfall, or low tide.

ORETI: *o:* the place of; *reti:* a snare.

OREWA: *o:* the place of; *rewa:* the rewa shrub.

ORIKAKA: *ori:* to wave to and fro; *kaka:* native parrot. To wave to attract the kaka. One method of snaring the kaka was to wave a piece of coloured fabric to attract the attention of the inquisitive bird, which was then easily caught. The Orikaka River was a noted place for birds.

ORIKARORO: *ori:* bad weather; *karoro:* seagull. Where seagulls congregate in bad weather.

ORINGI: the place of Ringi (Rangi). The inhabitants of a besieged pa included a beautiful young woman who was admired by Takarangi of another tribe. When he heard that the defenders were short of water he walked boldly to the palisades with a calabash of water for the young woman. This ultimately brought peace, and joy to the lovers. At the spring there was once a sign which read, "Kote Puna Oringi" (being the spring of Ringi).

Other places of this name probably mean *o:* the place of; *ringi:* to pour out. The place of pouring out. Orini has the same meaning.

ORINI: See Oringi.

ORONGO: *o:* the place of; *rongo:* round bay.

ORONGORONGO: Correctly Te Wai-o-Rongorongo: *te:* the; *wai:* water, or stream; *o:* of; *Rongorongo:* the name of a woman. The stream of Rongorongo.

OROPI: *o:* the place of; *ropi:* to cover up. The place of concealment. It may also be a Maori form of Europe.

OROROA: *o:* the place of; *roroa:* a shellfish.

OROTORE: *o:* the place of; *roto:* inside; *re* (short for *repo*): swamp. The swamp dwellers. This was an almost humorous term applied to the Maoris who lived along the banks of the River Avon in Christchurch. Although they lived in a swampy region they were well provided with eels and ducks.

OROTOREPO: See Orotore.

OROWAITI: see Orawaite. The Maoris, when referring to Reuben Waite, may have called him Oro Waite: old Waite. Another explanation is that the name may originally have been Ora-iti: escaping with difficulty.

ORUA: *o:* the place of; *rua:* a pit.

ORUAITI: *o:* the place of; *rua:* pit; *iti:* little. The place of the little pit.

ORUAIWI: *o:* the place of; *rua:* two, or pit; *iwi:* bone. The place of two bones, or The place of the pit containing bones.

ORUANUI: *o:* the place of; *rua:* pit; *nui:* big. The place of the large pit.

ORUAWAIRUA: *o:* the

Ruru: morepork

place of; *rua:* two; *wairua:* soul, or spirit. The place of the two spirits.

ORURU: *o:* the place of; *ruru:* morepork.

ORURUTUMARO: the immovable owl, the legendary name of a guardian of cultivations.

OTAGO: Correctly Otakou; *o:* the place of; *takou:* red earth, or red ochre. The Otago Peninsula abounded in yellow earth which yielded red ochre when burnt. The southern pronunciation of "k" approaches "g" in sound, and was pronounced Otago by the whalers. The name was extended from the Kaik near Taiaroa Head to the harbour, and finally to the province.

OTAHEIITI: the place of the little calabash.

OTAHU: *o:* the place of; *tahu:* signal fire. The local Maoris used to light fires on the peak to warn their neighbours of the approach of raiding parties.

OTAHUHU: *ota:* uncooked; *huhu:* grub. Eating of the huhu grub in an uncooked state. This was done by Waikato Maoris who, on dragging their canoes across the portage, discovered several rotten tree trunks full of huhu grubs.

OTAHUTI: *ota:* uncooked; *huti:* to pull out of ground.

OTAIKA: *o:* the place of; *taika:* to lie in a heap; or *ota:* to eat raw; *ika:* fish.

OTAKARO: *o:* the place of; *takaro:* games or sports. The place of the sport. The original name of the Avon River, and the site of Hagley Park.

OTAKI: *o:* the place of; *taki:* to stick in. The place where the staff was stuck in the ground by Hau, who was pursuing his wife.

OTAKIRI: *o:* the place of; *takiri:* loosening, or making free of tapu.

OTAKU: *o:* the place of; *taku:* slow and deliberate, or firm and solid.

OTAKUWAO: the place

where a bird was seen flying past a belt of trees.

OTAMAHUA : *o:* the place of; *tama* (short for *tamariki*) : children; *hua:* eggs. The place where children ate seagulls' eggs. This was the Maori name for Quail Island, where the gulls' eggs were a delicacy much esteemed by children as well as adults.

OTAMANGO : *ota:* uncooked; *mango:* shark.

OTAMARAKAU : *o:* the place of; *tamarakau:* warriors, or the young men who carry weapons.

OTAMARAU : *o:* the place of; *Tamarau:* a legendary spirit who comes in whirlwinds.

OTAMATAPIO : *ota:* uncooked; *mata:* a plant; *pio:* many.

OTANAMOMO: Correctly, Otanemoamoa. *o:* the place of; *tane:* man; *moamoa:* spherical stone.

OTANE : the moon on the 27th day, or, The place of man.

OTANENUI : *o:* the place of; *tane:* man; *nui:* big. The place of the big man.

OTANEURU : *o:* the place of; *tane:* man; *uru:* to gather berries. The place where the man gathered berries.

OTANGAROA : *o:* the place of; *Tangaroa:* god of the sea.

OTANGIHAKU : *o:* the place of; *tangi:* to cry or lament; *haku:* to murmur.

OTANGIWAI : *o:* the place of; *tangi:* to sound, or weep; *wai:* water. The place of sounding or weeping waters.

OTARA : *o:* the place of; *tara:* mountain peak, or spear.

OTARAIA : the place of Taraia, a Waitaha chief.

OTARI : *o:* the place of; *tari:* snare. The place of bird snares. Wilton and Mount Tinakori were noted places for birds.

OTATARA : *o:* the place of; *tatara:* to untie or loosen. Or *ota:* unripe; *tara:* point. Green point has been suggested as the meaning, but is unlikely.

OTAUA : *o:* the place of; *taua:* war-party.

OTAUTAHI : *o:* the place of; *Tautahi:* short for a personal name, Te Potiki-tautahi. A name for the River Avon.

OTAUTAU : the place of Tautau. Literally, *o:* the place of; *tautau:* greenstone earpendant with curved lower end.

OTAUTU : *ota:* raw; *utu:* revenge. Raw revenge. After a battle fought to avenge a wrong, the victors ate the bodies of the vanquished raw.

OTAWA : *o:* the place of; *tawa:* native tree. The place of tawa trees.

OTEKAIEKE : *o:* of; *te:* the; *kaieke:* going around.

OTEKURA : *o:* the place of; *te:* the; *kura:* red feather. The place of the red feather.

OTEMATATA : the place of good quartz or flint.

OTEPOPO : the place of Te Popo. Literally, the place of the decay.

OTEPOTI : *o:* the place of; *te:* the; *poti:* corner, angle. The place situated at a corner. The name of a village near the present Exchange, Dunedin.

OTETI : *o:* the place of; *te:* the; *ti:* cabbage tree. The place of the cabbage-tree.

OTEUKU : *o:* the place of; *te:* the; *uku:* white clay.

OTEWA : *o:* the place of; *te:* the; *wa:* open country.

OTIAKE : Properly Otiaki. *o:* the place of; *tiaki:* to watch for. The place of watching.

OTIKI : the place of the *tiki* (image) of Marokura.

OTIPUA : *o:* the place of; *tipua:* goblin.

OTIRA : *o:* the place of; *tira:* a company of travellers. There was an old camping place on the Otira River where food was prepared for the journey over the ranges by the Hurunui Pass.

Toroa: albatross

OTIRIA : *o:* the place of; *tiria:* to be planted.

OTITAHA: *o:* the place of; *titaha:* the axe.

OTOKIA : the place of Tokia. Literally, *o:* the place of; *tokia:* to be wet.

OTOKO : *o:* the place of; *toko:* a stick.

OTONGA : *o:* the place of; *tonga:* the south.

OTOROA : the place of Toroa.

OTOROHANGA : *o:* food for a journey; *torohanga:* to cause to extend over a distance. Food eked out. A chief who was going to Taupo carried only a small quantity of food which he made last out the journey by means of magic spells.

OTOTARA : *o:* the place of; *totara:* tree.

OTUHI : *o:* the place of; *tuhi:* smell of decaying fish.

OTUKOROITI : Correctly Okoroiti, the moon on the fifth day of the month. A fight that took place here began at sunrise on the fifth day and ended only when the moon rose.

OTUMAHANA : The place of warm, still waters.

OTUMOETAI : the tide standing still as if asleep.

OTUPAKA : *otu:* dried or scorched; *paka:* girdle.

OTUREHUA : *o:* the place of; *tu:* to stand; *rehua:* a star. The place where the summer star stands high in the heavens, i.e. a place where it is very warm.

OTUTAHANGA : *o:* the place of; *tu:* to stand; *tahanga:* naked. The place of standing naked.

OUE : the place of Ue or Ui who came to the South Island with Maui. Literally, a species of flax, or the moon on the fourth night.

OURUHIA : *o:* the place of; *uruhia:* to be attacked.

OWAHANGA : *o:* the place of; *wahanga:* the entrance. The mouth of the river.

OWAIRAKA : the place of Wairaka, or the water of Raka.

OWAIROA : *o:* the place of; *wai:* water; *roa:* long. The place of the long river, the old name for Howick.

OWAKA : *o:* the place of; *waka:* canoe, or trough.

OWANANGA : the place of the historical recitals.

OWE : *o:* the place of; *Wi* or *We* who came to the South Island with Maui.

OWEKA : *o:* the place of; *weka:* woodhen. The place where the weka is plentiful.

OWHAKATIHI : *o:* the place of; *whakatihi:* to pile up in a heap. The sons of Tuwharetoa ranged over the Kaingaroa Plain in search of someone to attack, but when they met a party of Maoris they were defeated, and their bodies were piled up in a heap at the foot of a tree.

OWHANGO : *o:* the place

Waka: canoe

of; *whango:* hoarse or nasal sound.

OWHAROA : *o:* food for a journey; *wharoa:* lasting a long time. It has much the same meaning as Otorohanga.

OWHATA : *o:* the place of; *whata:* a food store.

OWHIRO : *o:* the place of; *whiro:* a moonless night, or the god of darkness.

OWHITIANGATERA : *o:* of; *whitianga:* shining; *te:* the; *ra:* sun. The place of the shining sun.

P

PA : fortified village. The name usually occurs in places named by the Pakeha, such as Pa Flat.

PAEHINAHINA : *pae:* headland; *hinahina:* whitey-wood. Headland clothed with hinahina, mahoe, or whitey-wood trees.

PAEKAKARIKI : *pae:* perch; *kakariki:* parakeet. The perch of parakeets. There is a legend that Hau, who was pursuing his wife, came to a barrier of rock at the south end of the beach, which gave the name to the place. He drove his *taiaha* into the cliff, made a hole through it, walked through, and came out the other side, where he found his wife.

PAEKOHU : the place of fogs.

PAENGA : boundary, or the margin of the kumara plantations.

PAENGAROA : *paenga:* boundary; *roa:* long. Long boundary or margin.

PAERATA : *pae:* ridge; *rata:* tree. The ridge of the rata tree. A large rata stood here for many years, most of the surrounding trees being puriri.

PAERAU : *pae:* step, or ridge; *rau:* a hundred, or many. A hundred ridges.

PAEROA : *pae:* ridge, or range; *roa:* long. Long mountain range.

PAETAWA : *pae:* bird-snare; *tawa:* native tree. The tawa tree containing a bird-snare.

PAEWHENUA : *pae:* dock, or long-rooted weed; *whenua:* country. Noxious weed country.

PAHARAKEKE : *pa:* fortified village; *harakeke:* flax. Pa near which flax grows.

PAHAU : beard, or the withered, drooping lower leaves of the cabbage tree.

PAHAUTANE : Correctly Pahau-taniwha. *pahau:* whale-bone; *taniwha:* large fish. A war party was retiring up the coast after a raid, and found to their dismay that their concealed food stores had been plundered. They camped for the night and the next morning found a school of blackfish stranded on the beach. In their hunger, they ate the flesh raw. *Taniwha* is used for fish such as large sharks, and whales, as well as for fabulous monsters.

PAHAUTEA : *pahau:* beard; *tea:* white. White beard.

PAHI : company of travellers.

PAHIA : slapped, or a preparation of mashed food.

PAHIATUA : *pahi:* resting place; *atua:* a god. The resting place of a god. A chief escaped from a fight, and was led by his *atua* on the flight till they came here and rested on the hill.

PAHITUA : *pahi:* company of travellers; *tua:* cut down. Party of travellers cut down.

PAHORO : *pa:* fortified village; *horo:* to evacuate. The pa that was hurriedly evacuated.

PAIATEPUKAHU : *pai:* good; *a:* of; *te:* the; *pukahu:* abundant. The place of good, abundant food.

PAIHIA : good here. It is believed to be a word of mixed origin. The Rev. Henry Williams came to New Zealand knowing only a few words of Maori, including *pai,* which means good. When they came to this place he turned to his companion, a Maori chief, and said, "Pai here." It is possible that the name should be Pahia.

PAIRE : a bundle.

PAKARAE : *pa:* fortified village; *karae:* sea-bird. Seabird village.

PAKARAKA : *pa:* fortified village; *karaka:* native tree. Village of the karaka tree.

PAKAWAU : *pa:* flock, or colony; *kawau:* shag. Colony of shags.

PAKEHA : *pa:* garden plot; *keha:* indigenous white turnip. Plot where the turnip grows. One explanation of the name Pakeha for a white man is that it is one whose skin is white like that of a turnip. There are other explanations which are not so polite.

PAKIHI : flat land, usually dried up and poor.

PAKIHIROA : *pakihi:* flat country; *roa:* long or broad. Large extent of pakihi.

PAKIHIKURA : *pakihi:* flat land; *kura:* red. Reddish coloured flat land.

PAKIPAKI : An abbreviation of Pakipaki-o-Hinetemoa. This high-born young woman came to a stream accompanied by her slave girl. After she had

82

bathed, her maid slapped (paki-paki) and massaged her body.

PAKIRA: bald head. Pakira-a-Hikawera was a place where a chief of this name was wearing a closely fitting hat of birds' feathers. Feeling hot, he took it off, and another chief exclaimed, "What a beautiful bald head you have!"

PAKIRI: to grin.

PAKOTAI: pako: to make a sudden sound; tai: the sea. Sudden sound from the sea.

PAKOWHAI: pa: fortified village; kowhai: native tree. The pa by the kowhai trees. Or pako: to glean; whai: to search for. To look for remnants of the crop after it has been harvested.

PAKU: a small quantity.

PAKURANGA: paku: small quantity; ranga: company of persons, or shoal of fish. A small company, or a small shoal of fish.

PAMAPURIA: the Maori pronunciation of Pamphyllia, a locality named by the Rev. Joseph Matthews Kaitaia.

PANGAIO: pa: fortified village; ngaio: native tree. Pa near the ngaio trees.

PANGATOTARA: panga: thrown; totara: native tree. Probably named because a totara log was left here after a flood.

PANGURU: to make a rumbling sound.

PANIA: the Pania Reef at Napier is named after a woman of the sea people who married a Maori chief.

PAPA-AROHA: papa: foundation; aroha: love, or affection. The foundation of love. A place which was a centre of meeting for many scattered sub-tribes.

PAPAHAOA: a variety of kumara.

PAPAHINAU: papa: undulating or nearly flat land; hinau: a native shrub. Flat where the hinau grows. Also known as Papahina, and Papahinu.

PAPAIOEA: popularly believed to mean, How beautiful it is! Another explanation is, papai: exceedingly good; oea: the beauty that comes on the water when dead bodies are soaked in it. The Rangitane people were said to soak the bodies of the slain in water before storing or eating them. This place is the site of Palmerston North.

PAPAITI: papa: flat; iti: little. Little flat.

PAPAKAIO: papa: flat; kaio (South Island form of ngaio): Ngaio flat.

PAPAKI: a cliff against which the waves beat.

PAPAKURA: *papa:* flat; *kura:* red. Level land of red soil.

PAPAMOA: *papa:* flat; *moa:* raised beds. Level land with raised plots for cultivation.

PAPANUI: big flat plain, or a stage in a tree used as a seat by a bird-snarer.

PAPARATA: *papa:* flat land; *rata:* native tree. Rata flat.

PAPAREKAREKA: *papa:* flat rock; *rekareka:* pleasant. The name would mean Pleasant flat, but is a bluff in North Otago.

PAPARIMU: *papa:* flat; *rimu:* native tree. Rimu flat.

PAPAROA: long flat rock, or large expanse of level land. Where the name occurs as a headland it means long, flat rocky point.

PAPATAWA: *papa:* flat; *tawa:* native tree. Tawa flat.

PAPATEA: Possibly named after the light-coloured papa-rock banks of the stream, or a torm for a chief who was not tattooed.

PAPATOETOE: *papa:* flat; *toetoe:* pampas grass. Toetoe flat.

PAPATOTARA: *papa:* flat; *totara:* native tree. Totara flat.

PAPATOWAI: *papa:* flat;

towai: native tree. Towai (or kamahi) flat.

PAPAWAI: *papa:* flat land; *wai:* water. Inundated land.

PAPAWEKA: *papa:* flat; *weka:* wood-hen. Weka run, or fowl run. It sometimes appears as Tapapaweka.

PAPONGA: *pa:* fortified village; *ponga:* fern. Pa by the fern trees.

PARA: a type of fern, or possibly swamp.

PARAHARAHA: The name comes from a pool of black mud in which flax fibre was dyed.

PARAHAKI: A corruption of Parahaka. The Parawhau tribe had a large pa on the summit. They were invaded and defeated, and the conquerors danced a haka of triumph, or else prior to inviting the Parawhau to surrender. Parahaka is a contraction of Parawhau and haka.

PARAHAU: windy place.

PARAKAI: *para:* fern-root; *kai:* food, or to eat.

PARAKAKAU: *para:* fern; *kakau:* stalk. Fern-stalk.

PARAKAO: dried kumara.

PARANUI: *para:* fern; *nui:* big, or plenty. Plenty of fern.

PARAPARA: name of a Maori. Literally, soft mud used in dying flax fibre.

PARAPARAUMU: *para-*

para: scraps, or waste fragments; *umu:* earth oven in which scraps of food were found. A hungry *taua* (war party) captured a village but found only fragments of food in the oven. An earlier name may have been Paraparamau, meaning First-fruits for you.

PARAROA: Possibly should be Paraoa, as it is said that it means whale, because one was washed ashore here long ago.

PARATETAITONGA: dregs from the southern seas.

PARAU : slave.

PARAWA : *pa:* fortified village; *rawa:* property, or ground. Land on which the village was built.

PARAWAI : a cloak, or sandal. The name comes from Tahiti and was given by Tama-te-kapua to his kumara plantation in memory of those at Tahiti.

PAREKAKARIKI : *pare:* plume; *kakariki:* parakeet. Plume of the kakariki.

PAREKURA : red ornamental band for the forehead.

PAREMATA : a return feast for one previously given.

PAREMOREMO : hesitating, or slippery.

PARENGA : properly Perongo, slippery, or stream with slippery banks.

PARENGARENGA : the renga lily, or the place where the lily grows.

PAREORA : life-giving, or bountiful. The name may originally have been Pureora, a sacred rite performed for the recovery of the sick.

PARERA : native duck.

PARETAI : bank of a river.

PARIAWHAKATAHA-KURA : *pari:* cliff; *a:* of; *whakataka:* to cause to change direction; *kura:* red. The red lichen - covered cliff which causes the river to change direction.

PARIHAKA : low cliff.

PARIKARAKARAKA : echoing cliff.

PARIKAWA : Abbreviated form of Parikawakawa. *pari:* cliff; *kawakawa:* native tree. Cliff where the kawakawa grows.

PARIKAWAU : *pari:* cliff; *kawau:* shag. Shag cliff.

PARINGA : *pa:* blow; *ringa:* hand. To strike a blow with the hand.

PARININIHI : *pari:* cliff; *ninihi:* lofty. Lofty cliff. The White Cliffs were 800 feet in height.

PARINUIOTERA : *pari:* cliff; *nui:* big; *o:* of; *te:* the; *ra:* sun. The big cliff shining in the sun.

PARIPARI : precipitous country.

PARIROA : *pari:* cliff; *roa:* long, or tall. High cliff.

PARIRURU : *pari:* cliff; *ruru:* sheltered. Cliff which provides a shelter from the wind.

PARITEA : *pari:* cliff; *tea:* white. White or light-coloured cliff.

PARITUTU : *pari:* cliff; *tutu:* erect. Upright cliff.

PARIWHERO : *pari:* cliff; *whero:* red. Red cliff.

PAROA : *pa:* fortified village : *roa:* long. Spread out or straggling settlement.

PARORE : gentle, or friendly. Named after Parore te Awha who died in 1887 when he was nearly 100; he he was always friendly to the Pakeha.

PARUA : *pa:* fortified village; *rua:* pit, or two. Two pas, or the pit in the pa.

PARUAUKU : soil of white clay.

PARUPARU : black mud used in dying flax fibre.

PATARA : Maori pronunciation of Butler (or bottle).

PATEA: Name in full, Pateanui-a-Turi. The place where Turi's people threw down their great burdens.

PATEAROA : Long fortification with a clear view (Pawatea roa).

PATERANGI : *pa:* fortified

Pataka: raised storehouse

village; *te:* the; *rangi:* sky. The fort in the sky.

PATETONGA : *pa:* fortified village; *tonga:* south wind. Village swept by the south wind.

PATOKA : the pa in the rocks. The hill above the pa has great limestone formations.

PATUMAHOE : *patu:* weapon, or to strike; *mahoe:* timber of a native tree. In a battle at this place a chief was killed with a mahoe stake.

PATUNGA : *pa:* fortified village; *tunga:* circumstance of being wounded. The place where someone was wounded.

PATURUAHINE : *patu:* to strike; *ruahine:* old woman. The place where the old woman was struck.

PATUTAHI : *pa:* fortified

86

village; *tutahi:* lonely. Lonely or isolated village.

PAUA : shell-fish.

PAUATAHANUI : big shell-fish.

PEHU : variety of kumara, to pound, or to bend.

PEKA : named after Peka Makarini (Baker McLean).

PEKAPEKARAU : *pekapeka:* native bat; *rau:* many. The place where native bats were plentiful.

PEKATAHI: *peka:* branch; *tahi:* single. The single branch.

PEKERANGI : the outer palisades of a pa.

PEOWHAIRANGI : the Maori's attempt to pronounce Bay of Islands.

PEPEKE : native butterfly.

PERAKI : Probably Pireka (which was the spelling adopted by the French), fern, the root of which had a pleasant smell when pounded.

PERIA : Maori form of the Biblical Berea.

PETANE : Maori pronunciation of Bethany. The accent is on the first syllable. The name is now changed to Bay View to avoid confusion with Petone.

PETEREHEMA : Maori form of Bethlehem.

PETONE : a corruption of Pito-one. *pito:* end; *one:* sandy beach. End of the beach.

PIAKA : root of a tree, or

weapon made from a root.

PIAKO : shrunk, or hollow. The name was brought from Hawaiki by the Tainui people.

PIHA : ripple at the bow of a canoe.

PIHAMA : after Hone Pihama. Literally, *piha:* ripple; *ma:* white.

PIHANGA : window. The mountain had an opening in its side like the smoke vent in a house.

PIHAUTEA : *pihau:* a breakwind; *tea:* white.

PIKARORO : *pi:* nestling; *karoro:* sea-gull. Nestling of sea-gulls.

PIKOPIKO : winding.

PIKOWAI : *piko:* curving; *wai:* water. Curving stream.

PININOA : a refuge, or hiding place.

PIOPIO : native thrush.

PIOPIOTAHI : *piopio:* thrush; *tahi:* single. A single thrush. This was the Maori name for Milford Sound. A legend says that after Maui was defeated by the goddess of death, the thrush fled here sorrowing for its dead companion. Another legend says it is the name of a very early canoe.

PIPI : shell-fish.

PIPIKARITA : shell-fish for evil spirits.

PIPIRIKI : *pipi:* shell-fish;

riki: little. Little pipis. An old chief who was dying asked for little pipis, and a canoe was sent to get them, but by the time they arrived he was dead.

PIPIROA : *pipi:* shell-fish; *roa:* long, or many. Plenty of pipis.

PIPITEA : *pipi:* shell-fish; *tea:* white. White shell-fish.

PIPIWAI : damp, or swampy.

PIPIWHARAUROA : the shining cuckoo.

PIRIAKA : *piri:* to cling; *aka:* vine. The clinging forest vines.

PIRINOA : a parasitic plant.

PIRIPAI : the Maori form of Philippi.

PIRIPAUA : *piri:* clinging; *paua:* shell-fish. The clinging shell-fish. They are found in plenty in the two places in Marlborough with this name.

PIRIPIRI : a bur, commonly known as biddybid.

PIRONGIA: The full name is Pirongia-te-aroaro-o-Kahu, meaning the health-restoring purification of Kahurere whose husband restored her to health.

POHANGINA : the warming of the ovens at night.

POHATUROA : *pohatu:* stone; *roa:* long. Long stones are found in the river bed in

Westland. Elsewhere it means The tall rock.

POHOKURA : the name of a chief. Literally, *poho:* breast; *kura:* red.

POHONUI : the big haul.

POHOWAHINE : *poho:* breast; *wahine:* woman. A woman's breast.

POHOWAIKAWA : *poho:* breast; *waikawa:* bitter water.

POHUEHUE : climbing plant, such as convolvulus.

POHUENUI : *pohue:* convolvulus; *nui:* big, or many. Plenty of convolvulus.

POHUTU : splashing. The famous geyser at Whakarewarewa.

POHUTUKAWA : native tree with scarlet blossoms. The name usually given by the Pakeha, as in Pohutukawa Flat.

POKA : the name of a pet lizard lost at this place by Tamatea.

POKAIKOKO : flock of tuis.

POKAIWHENUA : a wanderer across the land. It is a tributary of the Waikato River.

POKAKA : a tree related to the hinau.

POKAPU : middle, or a house with the door in the middle of its side wall.

POKENO : turbid; or *po:*

88

night; *keno:* underworld. Night in the underworld.

POKERE : pulp of the tawa berry, or pitfall, or in the dark.

POKOHIWI : name of a chief. Literally, shoulder.

POKOPOKOIERE : native frog.

POKORORO : abbreviation for upokororo : native fish (grayling).

POMAHAKA : Correctly Pou-mahaka : posts to which snares are attached.

POMARE : named after Sir Maui Pomare.

PONEKE : Maori form of Port Nick, a contraction of Port Nicholson.

PONGA : tree-fern.

PONGAKAWA : to devour. Also *ponga:* tree-fern; *kawa:* bitter.

PONGAROA : name of a game; or, *ponga:* tree-fern; *roa:* long, or many. Plenty of tree-ferns.

PONUI : *po:* night; *nui:* big. Big night.

POPOIA : a gathering together.

POPOTUNOA : Properly Poupoutunoa, a post set up to mark the boundaries between Ngati-Mamoe and Ngai-Tahu.

PORANGAHAU : *po:* night; *rangahau:* pursuit. The inhabitants of Heretaunga once had to make a hasty retreat from their enemies to this place.

PORANGARUA : The correct form of the name is Pungarehu, ashes left by the fire. Some fugitives were discovered here when the wind stirred up the ashes of their fire.

PORANGIRANGI : to annoy at night.

PORANUI : *pora:* flat-roofed; *nui:* big.

PORARARI : Correctly, Pororari. *poro:* broken off; *rari:* uproar. The end of the uproar. The waters of the river would rise swiftly and turbulently, and recede as quickly.

POREWA : elevated platform or watch-tower.

PORIRUA : The proper form is probably Parirua. *pari:* flowing tide; *rua:* two. There are two arms in the harbour. It may also be named after the *taniwha* which was

Poneke: Port Nicholson

supposed to inhabit it.

PORO-O-TARAO : the posterior of Tarao. The chief was climbing the range ahead of his companions with his *rapaki* (waist-mat) kilted up, and the sight amused his companions who were below him.

POROPORO : a plant with a blue flower.

POROTI : a forest bird, or *poro:* to cut short; *ti:* cabbage tree.

POTAKA : after Utiku Potaka. Literally, a spinning top.

POTERITERI : dripping wet. Or Poutiritiri, a post on which offerings are hung, which is the more likely meaning.

POTERIWHI : port of relief.

POTETE : a small bark basket.

POUAKAI : a fabulous gigantic bird.

POUKAWA : *pou:* post; *kawa:* lean. Lean pole. Of the two chiefs who lived by the lake, one was more powerful than the other. The lesser chief asked that their fishing boundaries be divided, but the great chief was insulted. Then the lesser chief put a pole dividing the boundary, giving himself the best part of the lake, and leaving the *tuna kawa* (lean eels) for the other. The lake was then called lean pole. Much strife followed.

POUKINO : *pou:* post; *kino:* bad.

POUNAMU : greenstone.

POUNAWEA : *pou:* post; *nawea:* to set on fire. Post which was set on fire.

POUTINI: a form of greenstone. It is the "fish" which Kupe brought with him from Hawaiki, and was once the name for the whole of the West Coast.

POUTO : to cut off.

POUTU : *pou:* staff; *tu:* to stand. Staff standing up. When Tamatea reached this place on the east side of Lake Taupo, he rested on his staff while he surveyed the district.

POWARU : *po:* night; *waru:* eight. Eight nights. Tamatea and his men dragged their canoe overland from the headwaters of the Whanganui to Lake Taupo. At this place they were unable to obtain provisions and had to go for eight days and nights without food.

PUAHA : mouth of a river.

PUATAI : foam of the sea.

PUHA : a war-song, or a wild vegetable.

PUHINUI : *puhi*: plumes; *nui:* big. Great plume at the bow of a canoe. It is also the name of a canoe, and the settlement near Papatoetoe. It is also an early name for Warkworth, where it means Great promise, i.e. engagement or betrothal.

PUHOI: slow water, so called because the tide is very slow in creeping up the river and making it navigable for canoes.

PUKAHA: spongy or swampy.

PUKAKI: head of the creek, or where the stream meets the tidal waters. Lake Pukaki may have this meaning, but there is a legend that Rakaihaitu (who scooped out the southern lakes) saw its bulging outlet and called it *pu:* heaped or bunched up, and *kaki:* neck.

PUKAPUKA: shrub with white leaves.

PUKARAMU: a clump of karamu trees.

PUKATEA: a native tree.

PUKEARUHE: *puke:* hill; *aruhe:* fern-root. Hill where fern-root may be found.

PUKEATUA: *puke:* hill; *atua:* god. The hill of the god.

PUKEHAPOPO: *puke:* hill; *hapopo:* corpse of an enemy. The hill of the enemy corpse. A name which comes from the Society Islands.

PUKEHIKI: *puke:* hill;

hiki: charm to raise anything from the water. Hill of the incantation.

PUKEHINA: *puke:* hill; *hina (hinahina):* small tree, mahoe, or whiteywood. Hill of the mahoe tree.

PUKEHINAU: *puke:* hill; *hinau:* native tree. Hill of the hinau trees.

PUKEHIWITAHI: *puke:* hill; *hiwi:* peak; *tahi:* single. Hill with a single peak. It was named after the captain of the Arai-te-uru canoe, and is now known as Pukeviti.

PUKEHOU: *puke:* hill; *hou* (short for *houhou*): small flowering tree. Hill of the houhou trees. Pukehou in Horowhenua is the hill of dedication, where a boy was dedicated to the recovery of his tribal lands.

PUKEHUHU: *puke:* hill; *huhu:* grub. Hill where the huhu grubs were to be found.

PUKEHUIA: *puke:* hill; *huia:* extinct bird. Hill of the huias.

PUKEKAKARIKI: *puke:* hill; *kakariki:* parakeet. Hill of the parakeets.

PUKEKAHU: *puke:* hill; *kahu:* hawk. Hill of the hawks.

PUKEKAIHAU: *puke:* hill; *kaihau:* a ceremony performed over successful warriors when they return. Hill where victory is celebrated.

PUKEKAPIA : *puke:* hill; *kapia:* kauri gum. Kauri gum hill.

PUKEKARORO : *puke:* hill; *karoro:* seagull. Hill where the seagulls gather. It was fortified hill which frequently changed hands, and after each battle the seagulls gathered in their thousands.

PUKEKO : a swamp bird.

PUKEKOHE : *puke:* hill; *kohe (kohekohe):* a native tree. Hill where the kohekohe tree grows.

PUKEKOIKOI : *puke:* hill; *koikoi:* pointed. Pointed hills, or a sharp-ridged hill.

PUKEKOMA : *puke:* hill; *koma:* light-coloured. A hill that is light in colour.

PUKEKURA : *puke:* hill; *kura:* red. Red hill.

PUKEKURI : *puke:* hill; *kuri:* dog. Hill of dogs.

PUKEMAEROERO : *puke:* hill; *maeroero:* wild men. Hill of the wild men.

PUKEMAIRE : *puke:* hill; *maire:* native tree. Maire hill.

PUKEMAKARIRI : *puke:* hill; *makariri:* cold. Cold hill.

PUKEMAORI : *puke:* hill; *maori:* native. Maori hill.

PUKEMATA : *puke:* hill; *mata:* headland. The hill on the headland.

PUKEMATAWAI : *puke:* hill; *matawai:* source of waters. The hill which is the source of several streams or rivers. This name was given in recent years because the hill in the Tararuas is the source of a number of rivers.

PUKEMIRO : *puke:* hill; *miro:* native tree. Miro hill.

PUKEMOA : *puke:* hill; *moa:* giant extinct bird. Moa hill. So named because it was a haunt of the moa long ago, as is shown by the presence of the bones.

PUKENAMU : *puke:* hill; *namu:* sandfly. Sandfly hill.

PUKENGERENGERE : *puke:* hill; *ngerengere:* leprosy or skin disease. Hill where a sufferer from leprosy was segregated.

PUKENUI : *puke:* hill; *nui:* big. Big hill.

PUKEOKAOKA : *puke:* hill; *okaoko* (South Island form of *ongaonga*) : nettle. Hill where the nettles grow.

PUKEONE : *puke:* hill; *one:* sand. Sandy-topped hill.

PUKEOWARA : *puke:* hill; *o:* of; *wara:* Ward. Named after Sir Joseph Ward.

PUKEPOTO : dark blue earth used as a pigment. It is found in the nearby swamp.

PUKERANGI : *puke:* hill; *rangi:* sky. Hill that reaches up into the sky.

PUKERAU : *puke:* hill; *rau:* many. Many hills.

PUKERAUARUHE: *puke:* hill or mound; *rau:* many; *aruhe:* fern-root. A great heap of fern-root.

PUKERIMU : *puke:* hill; *rimu:* native tree. Rimu hill.

PUKEROA : *puke:* hill; *roa:* long. Long hill.

PUKERUA : *puke:* hill; *rua:* two. Two hills.

PUKETA : *puke:* hill; *ta:* sloping. Sloping hill. It is possible that the name is a corruption of *peketa:* dart.

PUKETAI : the hill of Tai. Literally, *puke:* hill; *tai:* sea. It may mean Hill across the water. Puketai, which is the site of Andersons Bay, Dunedin, should be Puketahi, The first hill, i.e. the first of a series of hills down the Peninsula.

PUKETAPU : *puke:* hill; *tapu:* sacred. Sacred or forbidden hill.

PUKETARATA : *puke:* hill; *tarata:* native tree. Lemonwood tree hill.

PUKETAWAI : *puke:* hill; *tawai:* native tree. Tawai hill.

PUKETERAKI : *puke:* hill; *te:* the; *raki* (South Island for of *rangi*) : sky. Hill reaching up to the sky. The proper form of the name is Puketiraki, *tiraki* meaning, lifting sharply skywards.

PUKETIHI : *puke:* hill; *tihi:* top. Top of the hill. From this peak the three mountains of National Park are seen on a clear day.

PUKETIRO : *puke:* hill; *tiro:* view. Hill with an extensive view from the summit.

PUKETITIRO : *puke:* hill; *titiro:* view. Hill with a commanding view.

PUKETOI : *puke:* hill; *toi:* summit. Summit of the hill.

PUKETONA : *puke:* hill; *tona:* mound.

PUKETOTARA : *puke:* hill; *totara:* native tree. Totara hill.

PUKETUI : *puke:* hill; *tui:* native bird. Tui hill.

PUKETUTU : *puke:* hill; *tutu:* native tree. Tutu hill. There are several places of this name, and in some, as in Weeks Island, *tutu* is the tree; in others it is a plant.

PUKEURI : named after a woman on the Arai-te-uru canoe. Literally *puke:* hill; *uri:* dark. Dark hill.

PUKEWAHIA : firewood hill. Literally *puke:* hill; *wahia:* split, or divided. Split hill.

PUKEWHERO: *puke:* hill; *whero:* red. Red hill. Named by a party in 1932 because the last few hundred feet are a jumble of bright red rocks.

PUKOROKIO : a bunch of

koromiko. It is said that here, near Riverton, the moa was killed. Koromiko was the wood traditionally used for cooking the moa. The name of the stream has now been changed to Moa Creek.

PUKU: named after a woman carried away by the maeroero. Literally, belly.

PUKURAHI: *puku:* belly; *rahi:* big. Big belly.

PUKUTAHI: named for a chief who was killed at Lake Te Anau. Literally, *puku:* belly; *tahi:* single.

PUNAKAIKI: *puna:* a spring; *kaiki* (a mis-spelling of *kaike* or *kaika*) : to lie in a heap. This is the site of the famous pancake rocks, which lie in heaps, and the "spring" is no doubt the blow-hole. But there was a Ngai-Tahu belief that Punakaiki is a word that describes the neck and throat of a human being, the rock and blow-holes being likened to them.

PUNAKITERE: swiftly flowing spring.

PUNAPITO: *puna:* spring; *pito:* end. End of the spring.

PUNARUKU: *puna:* spring; *ruku:* to sink or dive. To sink into a spring. The name has been brought from Hawaiki.

PUNGANUI: a corrupt form of Ponganui, a large tree-fern.

PUNGAREHU: ashes.

PUNI: the encampment, or to be blocked up.

PUNIHO: ambush.

PUNIU: fern.

PUNIWHAKAU: *puni:* camp; *whakau:* to arrive. To reach camp.

PUPONGA: hunched up.

PUPU: The name for the largest fresh-water spring in the world at Takaka is sadly misnamed. Properly it was known to the Maoris as Waikaremumu, which could be rendered Boisterous wind that ruffled the waters. It was shortened by the Pakeha to Mumu and possibly corrupted to Bubu; but the Bubu diggings were some miles away. The name was given to the springs, and it was thought that the original Maori must have been Pupu.

The Pupu Stream in Marlborough is named after a shell-fish.

PUPUKE: The name in full is Pupuke-mo'ana, the over-flowing lake.

PURAKANUI: Correctly Purakaunui. *pu:* heap; *rakau:* timber; *nui:* big. Big heap of firewood. The inhabitants of Goat Island were slaughtered in tribal warfare and their

94

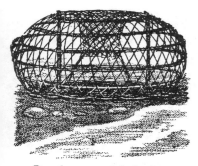

Puraka: crayfish basket

bodies put in a great pile like a heap of firewood.

PURAMAHOI: *pura:* to twinkle or shine; *mahoi:* steadily. To shine steadily.

PURANGI: a bag net for catching lampreys. Such nets were totally enclosed except for a narrow opening, and this place was a clearing in the bush with a similar appearance.

PURAU: a spear or fork. It may have had some connection with a traditional mussel basket.

PUREHUA: a moth.

PUREKIREKI: tufts of grass, or a heap of fragments.

PUREORA: a sacred rite performed for the recovery of the sick.

PURERUA: *pure:* to set free from tapu; *rua:* two.

PUREWA: to float.

PURIRI: native tree. The place was named because the puriris grew so plentifully.

PURU: full, or a plug.

PUTANGAHAU: Possibly a shortened form of Te Putangaotehau, the place where the wind comes from.

PUTAREPO: the place at the end of the swamp where it could be crossed.

PUTARINGAMOTU: the place of the severed ear. It was a figurative expression for an isolated patch of bush, the site of Riccarton.

PUTARURU: Correctly Putaaruru; *puta:* hole, or to appear; *a:* after the manner of; *ruru:* owl, or morepork. The nest or hole of a morepork, which is often found in a hollow tree.

PUTIKI: In full, Putiki-whara-nui-a-Tamatea-pokai-whenua, the place where

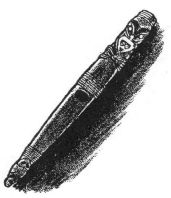

Putorino: flute

95

Tamatea the navigator tied his topknot with flax. Tamatea of the Takitimu canoe went ashore at Whanganui and had his hair dressed. The slave procured flax, but it was rotten and broke. Tamatea said it was not like the *wharanui* (a kind of flax) obtained on the East Coast. The place was named after the incident.

PUTORINO : flute.

PUWERA : warm.

R

RAETIHI : *rae:* headland; *tihi:* summit. Prominent summit.

RAHIRI : to welcome.

RAHOTU : *ra:* sun; *hotu:* to long for. To long for the sun.

RAHUI : boundary post. In full, Pou-rahui. It also means a sanctuary.

RAI : ribbed, or furrowed. It probably should be *rae:* headland.

RAKAIA : adorned. It is probably the South Island form of *rangaia:* to arrange in ranks, and refers to the need for strong men to stand in ranks to break the force of the current for the weaker ones when attempting to ford the river.

RAKANUI : Properly Ra-kaunui : *rakau:* tree; *nui:* big. Big tree.

RAKAU : tree, or timber.

RAKAUHAUKA : *rakau:* wood, or tree; *hauka* (South Island form of *haunga*) : to smell.

RAKAUHAUNGA : See Rakauhauka.

RAKAUNUI : *rakau:* tree; *nui:* big, or many. Big tree, or many trees.

RAKAUROA : *rakau:* tree; *roa:* long. Tall tree.

RAKAUTAO : *rakau:* timber; *tao:* spear. Wood for making spears.

RAKIURA : *raki* (South Island form of *rangi*) : sky; *ura:* glowing. Glowing sky. The Maori name for Stewart Island. There is another tale that a young chief wished to marry but arrived just too late, for the young woman was already wedded. The name in full is Te Ura o Te Raki-tamau, the blushing of Te Raki-tamau.

RAMAIKU : Maori form of Damascus.

RAMARAMA : a native tree.

RANANA : Maori form of London.

RANGANUI : *ranga:* parade; *nui:* big. A long line of warriors.

RANGATAUA : a grasshopper; or *ranga:* line of warriors; *taua:* war party. Warriors drawn up in ranks.

RANGATIRA : chief.

RANGAUNU : *ranga:* shoal of fish; *unu:* to pull out. Good fishing.

RANGIAHUA : great; or to approach the sky.

RANGIAOWHIA : *rangi:* sky; *aowhia:* clouded. Clouded sky.

RANGIATEA : Short for Rangiatea-te-tuahu-o-Io-mata-kanakana : the shrine of Io of the far-seeing eyes. A sacred name which came from Hawaiki.

RANGIHAEATA : the first rays of morning light.

RANGIAWHIA : See Rangiaowhia.

RANGIHOUA : named after a chief of long ago.

RANGIKURA : *rangi:* sky; *kura:* red. Red sky. The original name was Whenuakura, red land.

RANGIORA: good weather after a bad spell, or an invalid getting better, or day of peace. In the North Island it refers to a shrub.

RANGIOTU : the day of the god of war.

RANGIPO : *rangi:* sky; *po:* night. The place where the sky is dark, a reference to the time when Ngatoro-i-rangi called down fire on his enemies.

RANGIPUTA : *rangi:* sky; *puta:* to pass through. To cross the sky.

RANGIRIRI : *rangi:* sky; *riri:* angry. The angry sky.

RANGITAIKI : *rangi:* chief; *tai:* tide; *ki:* full. A great river like a full tide.

RANGITATA : *rangi:* sky, or day; *tata:* lowering clouds. A day of lowering clouds.

RANGITIKEI : *rangi:* sky, or day; *tikei:* to stretch the legs. The day of striding out. It may also refer to a ford which was crossed by walking on tip-toes.

RANGITOTO : *rangi:* sky, or day; *toto:* blood. A common name in New Zealand, usually imported from Hawaiki. Rangi-toto Island, Auckland, is in full, Nga Rangi-i-totongia-a-Tama-te-kapua, the days of the bleeding of Tama-te-kapua.

Arawa Canoe

The famous chief of the Arawa canoe was badly wounded here.

RANGITUKIA : *rangi:* day; *tukia:* to be attacked. The day of the attack.

RANGIURU : *rangi:* sky; *uru:* west. The western sky.

RANGIWAHIA : *rangi:* sky; *wahia:* to split. Break through which the sky can be seen, or a glimpse of heaven. A party of travellers came either to a clearing, or to a moment when there was a rift in the clouds.

RANUI : *ra:* sun; *nui:* many. Plenty of sunshine. A modern name.

RAORIKIA : Maori form of Laodicea.

RAPAHOE : paddle blade.

RAPAKI : kilt. When the chief Te Rangiwhakaputa took possession, he put down his kilt to mark his ownership.

RAPAURA: running waters.

RAROA : *ra:* day; *roa:* long. Named by Ihenga because he spent so many hours paddling his canoe.

RATA : a native tree.

RATANA : named after the Maori prophet.

RATANUI : *rata:* native tree; *nui:* many. Plenty of rata trees.

RAUKAWA : leaves of the kawakawa. They were worn by

Rapaki: kilt

a chief in mourning and thus gave the name of the Ngati-Raukawa tribe. Raukawa was the Maori name for Cook Strait.

RAUKUMARA : *rau:* leaf; *kumara:* sweet potato. Kumara leaves.

RAUMATI : summer.

RAUPO : native reed.

RAURIMU : *rau:* many, or leaf; *rimu:* red pine. Many rimus or Rimu leaf.

RAWENE : *ra:* day; *wene:* many. Many days.

RAWHITI : the place of the sunrise.

RAWHITIROA : *ra:* sun; *whiti:* to shine; *roa:* long. Long sunshine. It may also mean In the direct line of the sun, as the settlement ran from east to west.

REHIA : pleasure.

98

Raupo: New Zealand reed

REHUTAI : sea-spray.

REIKORANGI : the gate of heaven, or the breast of heaven. A slave of this name was buried here.

REINGA : the underworld.

REMUERA : Correctly Remuwera, the burnt edge of a flax garment.

REPO : swamp.

REPOROA : *repo:* swamp; *roa:* long. Long swamp.

RERE : waterfall.

RETARUKE : Correctly reretaruke. *rere:* waterfall; *taruke:* trap for crayfish.

REWA : to begin, or to meet.

REWANUI : *rewa:* mast; *nui:* big. Big mast.

REWAREWA : native tree.

RIKIRIKI : scattered.

RIMU : red pine.

RIMUNUI : *rimu:* native tree; *nui:* big, or many. Many rimus.

RIMURAPA : *rimu:* seaweed; *rapa:* to look for. The Maori name for Sinclair Head.

RIMUTAKA : Correctly Remutaka, to sit down to rest. An incident in the pursuit of his wife by Hau.

RIPA : Correct name is Ripapa. *ri:* flax rope; *papa:* flat rock. A canoe was tied by a flax rope to a rock on the island.

RIPONUI: *ripo:* whirlpool; *nui:* big. Big whirlpool.

RIWAKA : Correctly Riuwaka. *riu:* inside, or bulge; *waka:* canoe. The inside or bulge of a canoe.

ROHEPOTAE : *rohe:* rim; *potae:* hat. Rim of the hat, the term applied to the boundary of the King Country after the Maori Wars. The Kingite Maoris said that it was as if the hat had been taken away, leaving them only the rim.

ROMAHAPA : *roma:* stream, or channel; *hapa:* crooked. Crooked channel.

RONA : to bind, or swirling.

RONGOKOKAKO: *rongo:* to listen; *kokako:* native crow. Listening to the kokako. It may be named after the father of Tamatea.

RONGOTAI : *rongo:*

sound; *tai:* sea. The sound of the sea. A modern name.

RONGOTEA : probably named after a chief.

ROTO : lake.

ROTOAIRA : *roto:* lake; *a:* of; *Ira:* a person. The lake of Ira.

ROTOAKIWA : *roto:* lake; *a:* of; *Kiwa:* a person. The lake of Kiwa.

ROTOATARA : *roto:* lake; *a:* of; *Tara:* a chief. The lake of Tara who killed the *taniwha* that inhabited it. The lake is now dried up.

ROTOATUA : *roto:* lake; *atua:* god. The lake of the god.

ROTOEHU : *roto:* lake; *ehu:* turbid. Turbid lake.

ROTOITI : *roto:* lake; *iti:* little; Little lake. The name of the northern Rotoiti in full was Te Roto-iti-kite-a-Ihenga, the little lake seen or discovered by Ihenga.

ROTOKAHA : *roto:* lake; *kaha:* boundary. The boundary lake.

ROTOKAKAHI : *roto:* lake; *kakahi:* freshwater shellfish. The shell-fish were killed by the Tarawera eruption. The Green Lake.

ROTOKAWA : *roto:* lake; *kawa:* bitter. Lake of bitter waters.

ROTOKAWAU : *roto:* lake; *kawau:* shag. Shag lake.

ROTOKOHU : *roto:* lake; *kohu:* fog or mist. Misty lake.

ROTOMA : *roto:* lake; *ma:* clear. Lake of clear waters.

ROTOMAHANA : *roto:* lake; *mahana:* warm. Warm lake.

ROTOMAKARIRI : *roto:* lake; *makariri:* cold. Cold lake.

ROTOMANU : *roto:* lake; *manu:* bird. Lake of birds.

ROTONGARO: *roto:* lake; *ngaro:* lost, or hidden. Hidden lake.

ROTOROA : *roto:* lake; *roa:* long. Long lake.

ROTORUA : *roto:* lake; *rua:* two. The second lake. The full name was Rotorua-nui-a-Kahu. It was the second big lake to be discovered by Ihenga who named it after his father-in-law Kahu-mata-momoe.

ROTOTUNA : *roto:* lake; *tuna:* eel. Eel lake.

ROTOWARO : *roto:* lake; *waro:* live coals. A fire glowing by the lake-side.

ROTOWHERO : *roto:* lake; *whero:* red. Red lake, so called because of the oxide of iron deposits.

ROTOWHIO : *roto:* lake; *whio:* blue duck. Lake or pool of the blue duck.

ROTU : a sleep-making spell.

RUAHINE : a wise woman, or an old woman.

RUAKAKA: nesting place of the parakeets.

RUAKITURI: *ruaki:* to vomit; *turi:* knee, or post.

RUAKURA: *rua:* pit; *kura:* red. Pit in the red earth.

RUAKURI: *rua:* pit; *kuri:* dog. Cave of the dogs. Wild dogs were found living by the mouth of the cave.

RUAMAHANGA: *rua:* two; *mahanga:* fork. Twin forks. Hau discovered a drinking trough and a bird snare in the twin forks of a tree.

RUAMOKO: *rua:* pit or hole; *moko:* lizard. Home of the lizard.

RUAPEHU: *rua:* hole; *pehu:* to explode, or make a loud noise. Ruapehu has two vents or blow-holes from which steam is expelled.

RUAPEKAPEKA: *rua:* hole; *pekapeka:* native bat. The bat's nest. Thousands of bats lived in the hollows of trees.

RUAPUKE: *rua:* two; *puke:* hill. Two hills.

RUAROA: *rua:* pit; *roa:* long. Long pit.

RUATAHUNA: *rua:* two; or pit; *tahuna:* sandbank. Two sandbanks.

RUATANGATA: *rua:* pit; *tangata:* man. Cave in which people lived.

RUATANIWHA: *rua:* two; *taniwha:* water monster. Two great taniwhas once lived in the lake. They fought over a boy who fell in, and their struggles formed the Tukituki and Waipawa Rivers which drained the lake.

Other places with this name mean Taniwha pit or cave.

RUATAPU: *rua:* pit; *tapu:* sacred. Sacred cave.

RUATOKI: *rua:* pit, or two; *toki:* adze. Two adzes, or adze in the cave.

RUATORIA: Correctly Ruaatoria, kumara pit belonging to Toria.

RUAWAHIA: *rua:* pit; *wahia:* split. Gulch cleft by volcanic action.

RUAWAI: *rua:* pit, or two; *wai:* water. Water in a cave, or two streams.

RUAWARO: *rua:* cave; *waro:* live coals. Embers in a cave.

RUKUHI: the act of diving.

RUNANGA: an assembly.

RUNARUNA: a plant, or a game.

RURU: owl or morepork.

T

TAEMARO: *tae:* to dye; *maro:* apron. Dyed apron.

TAHAIA: *taha:* to pass,

on one side; *ia:* current. Passing along the slack water of the stream.

TAHAKOPA : *taha:* side; *kopa:* curved. Curved side.

TAHATIKA : coastline, or at the edge of the river.

TAHAWAI: *taha:* side; *wai:* sea. Seaside.

TAHEKE : waterfall.

TAHEKEAUA : *taheke:* waterfall; *aua:* herring. A place for catching herrings by the waterfall.

TAHEKEROA : long river rapid or cataract.

TAHORA: a clearing, or an expanse of open country.

TAHORAITI : little clearing.

TAHORAMAUREA : uncultivated, or covered with tussocks.

TAHUNA : sandbank or shoal.

TAHUNANUI : *tahuna:* sandbank; *nui:* many.

TAHURANGI : the first Maori to ascend Mount Egmont. Literally *tahu:* ridgepole; *rangi:* sky.

TAIAMAI: An old name for the Bay of Islands. In full it is Ka kata nga puriri o Taiamai, the puriri trees of Taiamai are laughing.

TAIAROA: named after the chief Taiaroa.

TAIERI : Properly Taiari :

tide on the eleventh night of the moon.

TAIHAPE Originally Otaihape : the place of Taihape. Literally *tai:* angle; *hape:* crooked.

TAIHARURU : *tai:* sea; *haruru:* resounding. Thundering sea.

TAIHOA : by and by.

TAIKIRAU : *taiki:* snag; *rau:* many. Many snags.

TAIKO : The name of a Maori, sometimes spelt Tycho. Literally rib or basket. See Tycho.

TAIKOREA : *tai:* sea; *korea:* small canoe. Small canoe on the sea.

TAINUI : one of the canoes of the migration. Literally *tai:* sea; *nui:* big. Great sea.

TAIOMA : white soil.

TAIPO : goblin, or devil. The river was given this name because when it was in flood it deserved the name. It is no doubt of modern origin.

TAIPOITI : little Taipo.

TAIPUHA : a very high tide.

TAIRUA : *tai:* tide; *rua:* two. Two tides, one from the north and the other from the south.

TAITA : driftwood in the bed of the river.

TAITAMAHINE : *tai:* sea; *tamahine:* girls. The sea of

girls—the peaceful east coast waters, compared with Taita-matane, the rough west coast, which was called the sea of men, where warriors, not girls, were needed to man the canoes.

TAITAMATANE : See Taitamahine.

TAI-TAPU : an obsolete word for boundary. Literally *tai*: tide; *tapu*: sacred.

TAITIMU : *tai*: tide; *timu*: ebb. Ebb tide.

TAKAHANGA : track or footpath.

TAKAHE : native bird, the notornis.

TAKAHIWAI : *takahi*: to tramp; *wai*: water. To trample into the water.

TAKAHUE : *taka*: heap; *hue*: gourd. Heap of gourds.

TAKAKA : bracken. A name which comes from the Society Islands.

TAKANINI : named after the friendly chief Ihaka Takaanini. Literally, *taka*: heap; *nini*: to glow.

TAKAPAU : flax sleeping mat. A pa in the far north was given this name because the people of Tainui put down a mat and went to sleep, i.e. they resided there for some time.

TAKAPU : gannet.

TAKAPUNA : *taka*: assembly; *puna*: spring. The gathering of people which

drank at the spring were Tainui men who were claiming possession of the land.

TAKAIRITAWA : to jerk out of the water. Thousands of ducks were caught in this way.

TAKIROA : *taki*: sound; *roa*: long. Echo. The name of the rock shelter at Waitaki where there are Maori paintings. There is very clear echo.

TAKITIMU : a famous canoe of the migration commanded by Tamatea. It was petrified in the form of the Takitumu or Takitimo Mountains.

TAKITUI : *taki*: to follow; *tui*: native bird. To follow the tui.

TAKIWA-WAIARIKI : *takiwa*: district; *waiariki*: hot springs. A general name for the thermal district.

TAKUTAI : *taku*: coast; *tai*: sea. Sea-coast.

TAMA-AHUA: the peak on Mount Egmont is named after the first Maori to ascend it.

TAMAHERE : *tama*: son; *here*: tie up.

TAMAKI : battle. The isthmus was *tamaki-whenua,* a contested land. It was known as Tamaki-makau-rau, Tama-ki of a hundred lovers.

TAMARAU : *tama*: son; *rau*: many. Many sons.

TANEATUA : the tohunga

(priest) of the Mataatua canoe. Literally, Tane the god.

TANEAUROA : named after an old chief. Literally, *tane:* man; *au:* whirlpool; *roa:* long. The man of the long rapid or whirlpool.

TANEKAHA : *tane:* man; *kaha:* strong. Strong man.

TANGIIHI : correctly Tangaehe : the noise of the rustling or murmuring tide. There are beds of shells on the foreshore and the waves ripple over them.

TANGAHOE : named by Turi after his paddle.

TANGARAKAU : fallen trees, referring to a great quantity of trees carried down by the river when in flood.

TANGIARO: In full Tangi-aro-o-Kahu. *tangi:* to weep; *aro:* desire for; *o:* of; *Kahu:* Kahu-mata-momoe. After the death of his father, Kahu-mata-momoe turned his face to Moehau where his father was buried, and chanted a lament of yearning and sorrow.

TANGIMOANA : *tangi:* lament; *moana:* ocean. The lament of the ocean.

TANGITERE : *tangi:* to cry or lament; *tere:* swiftly, or to float.

TANGITERORIA : *tangi:* to cry; *te:* the; *roria:* conch shell. The sound of the trum-

Tangiwai: a kind of greenstone

pet. Eel weirs were built on the Wairoa River, and as the Maoris paddled their canoes up to them the force of the water was audible and was likened to the sound of a conch shell being blown.

TANGIWAI : *tangi:* to weep or lament; *wai:* water. Weeping waters. Noted for its sudden floods which many years ago were responsible for the death of a chief, as they were for the terrible railway disaster in 1953. Fiordland greenstone is called tangiwai because of the flecks in it that resemble tears.

TANGOIO : *tango:* to take hold of; *io:* a strand of rope or lock of hair. To hold a strand of rope.

TANGOWAHINE : *tango:* to seize; *wahine:* woman. To abduct a woman.

TANIWHA : monster.

TAONUI : *tao:* spear; *nui:* big. Great spear.

TAOROA : *tao:* spear; *roa:* long. Long spear.

TAPANUI : Possibly a contraction of Te-tapuwae-o-Uenuku : the footprints of the rainbow god. Or literally, the great edge, referring to the edge of the forest. A third theory is that the name was originally Te Papanui, the great flat area of country.

TAPAWERA : *tapa:* edge; *wera:* hot, or burnt. The burnt fringe (of the forest).

TAPU : sacred. Usually given for a particular reason, as at Coromandel, where the great battle resulted in many dead being buried and making the place sacred; or as at Riwaka, where a tohunga placed a hair of his head near the doorway of his house to keep intruders away.

TAPUAEHARURU : *tapuae:* footsteps; *haruru:* sounding. The noise of footsteps, or resounding footsteps. At Taupo the name was given because of the caverns which caused footsteps to resound. Ihenga gave the name in Northland because of his own footsteps.

TAPUAENUKU : the footsteps of the rainbow god. In full, Tapuae-Uenuku.

TAPUHI : to nurse.

TAPUI : friend, or close companion.

TAPUWAE : footsteps, the place in Taranaki being named by Turi. Tapuwae, the site of the Wairoa P.O., was named by Sir James Carroll after a chief.

TAPUWAEHARURU : See Tapuaeharuru.

TAPUWAEROA : *tapuwae:* footsteps; *roa:* long. Long footsteps. They were made by the giant Rongokako, who left his footprints at Kidnappers, Mahia, and East Cape.

TARAKAI : *tara:* seabird; *kai:* to live. A place where seabirds nested.

TARAKOHE : *tara:* thorn; *kohe:* native plant.

TARAMAKAU : Possibly Teremakau; *tere:* to flow; *makau:* curve. Another interpretation is that it means *tere:* swift; *makau:* spouse, referring to a man who was in search of his absconding wife who turned to stone.

TARAMEA : spear grass.

TARANAKI : There have been many theories about this name. *Tara:* peak, presents no problems; *naki* may be *ngaki,* clear of vegetation. Probably

Taranaki was the tribal name given to Mount Egmont. A very old name was Pukehaupapa, ice mountain, and when referring to its graceful shape it was called Puke-o-naki.

TARARUA: *tara:* peak; *rua:* two. Two peaks. The double peaks of the Tararua Range are Pukeamoamo and Pukeahurangi opposite Otaki, both named by Rangi-kaikore (Rangi the foodless), because he broke two *tara* or bird spears while on the range.

TARATA: a native tree.

TARATAHI: *tara:* peak; *tahi:* single. Single peak—in this case Mount Holdsworth.

TARAWERA: *tara:* birdspear; *wera:* burnt. Hikawera of Hawke's Bay had a successful season killing birds, and left his spears in a hut. When he returned the next season he found that the hut and his spears had been burnt.

TAREHA: ochre.

TAREWA: The full name is Tarewa-pounamu; *tarewa:* to suspend; *pounamu:* greenstone. A greenstone ornament was hung on a tree as a sacred offering.

TARIKI: possibly Tarika, to toss about.

TARINGAMOTU: *taringa:* ear; *motu* (or *mutu*): cut off. Mutilated ear.

TARUKENGA: place of slaughter.

TATAIKOKO: *tatai:* to adorn; *koko:* pendant. The chief Pawa adorned himself at this place.

TATARA-A-KINA: *tatara:* spine; *a:* of; *kina:* sea-urchin. The spines of the sea-urchin. An old chief of Taupo compared this mountainous country to the sea-urchins of Heretaunga.

TATARAMOA: *tatara:* distant; *moa:* extinct bird. Distant moa.

TATARA: a species of shark.

TATU: to be content, or to touch bottom.

TATUANUI: *tatua:* girdle; *nui:* big. Large girdle.

TAUERU: hanging in clusters.

TAUHARA: isolated, alone. The mountain stands alone in the plain.

TAUHERENIKAU: Correctly Tauwharenikau, the overhanging nikau palms. When Hau was travelling in the Wairarapa he discovered a whare the walls and roof of which were thatched with nikau leaves.

TAUHOA: to befriend.

TAUKITUA: the further ridge.

TAUMARERE: to fall, or

a cord passed over the ridge-pole of a house. Possibly Taumariri, tranquil season.

TAUMARUNUI: *taumaru:* screen; *nui:* big. Huge screen. When the chief Pehi Taroa was dying he asked that a screen be erected to shade him from the sun. He died before the work was completed with the words taumaru nui on his lips.

TAUMATA : brow of a hill. This is a component of many place names.

TAUMATAWHAKATANGIHANGAKOAUAUOTAMATEAPOKAIWHENUAKITANATAHU : the brow of the hill where Tamatea who sailed all round the land played his nose flute to his lady love. There are several forms of this firmly established Maori name, reputed to be the longest in the country. Another form, broken into its component parts, is Te Taumata-okiokinga-whakatangihanga-o-te-koauau-a-Tamatea-pokai-whenua.

TAUOMA : Short for Tauomaoma, to race, or strive in running.

TAUPAKI : a loin-mat; or a season of fine weather.

TAUPARIKAKA : Correctly Tauparekaka; *taupare:* to blindfold; *kaka:* parrot. To blindfold a parrot. This was done to decoy kakas, which were fairly tame. It prevented them from flying away.

TAUPIRI : *tau:* ridge of hill; *piri:* to keep close to. It has been rendered, To clasp round the waist.

TAUPO : Short for Taupo-nui-a-Tia; *taupo:* shoulder-cloak; *nui:* big; *a:* of; *Tia:* the discoverer of the lake. The great cloak of Tia. Tia slept by the lake, and it has been conjectured that Taupo is a reference to his long sleep at night at that place.

TAURANGA : a sheltered anchorage, or a resting place for canoes.

TAURANGAKAWAU : *tauranga:* sheltered place; *kawau:* shag. A resting place for shags.

TAURANGA-KOHU: *tauranga:* resting place; *kohu:* mists. A place where the mists linger.

Tauranga: canoe anchorage

TAURANGA-MANGO : *tauranga:* landing place; *mango:* shark. Where the sharks were landed. The old name for Shelly Beach.

TAURAROA : *taura:* rope; *roa:* long. Long rope.

TAURARUA : *taura:* rope; *rua:* two. Two ropes. The Maori name for Judges Bay.

TAUREWA : having no settled home.

TAURIKO : A Pakeha-given name. Originally Tauri-co, standing for Tauranga Rimu Company. It was thought to be a misspelt Maori name and changed to Tauriko.

TAURIKURA : *tauri:* feather ornament; *kura:* red. Ornament of red feathers.

TAUTANE : *tau:* ridge of a hill; *tane:* man. Man on the ridge.

TAUTORO : to stretch forward.

TAUTUKU : to stoop, or to be at a loss.

TAUWHARANUI: *tau:* ridge of a hill; *wharanui:* a species of flax. Flax bushes on the ridge.

TAUWHARE: to overhang, or a shelter.

TAWA : a native tree.

TAWANUI : *tawa:* tree; *nui:* many. Plenty of tawa .trees.

TAWHAI : a native tree.

TAWHARANUI : *tawhara:* kiekie flowers; *nui:* many. Plenty of kiekie flowers.

TAWHITI : trap. This was a place where Pawa of the Bay of Plenty set a trap to catch Rongokako, the giant of Kahuranaki.

Tawhiti is a component of many place names, meaning Tahiti, and has been brought from the homeland of the Maori people.

TAWHITINUI : a forest in Tahiti.

TAWHIUAU : swirling mists.

TAWIRIKOHUKOHU : whirling mists. The mountain holds the clouds when the rest of the Tararua Range is clear.

TE AHI-A-MANONO : the flames of Manono. The site of part of Lower Hutt, and a name of great antiquity, as it was a description of the burning of a great house on Manono.

TE AHI-KAI-KOURA-A-TAMA-KI-TE-RANGI : the full name of Kaikoura, q.v.

TE AHI-MANAWA-A-TE-KOHIPIPI : The full name of the Ahimanawa Range, q.v.

TE AHI - PUPU - A - IHENGA : *te:* the; *ahi:* fire; *pupu:* mussel; *a:* of; *Ihenga:* the explorer. The fire at which mussels were cooked by Ihenga.

TE AHUAHU : *te:* the; *ahuahu:* mounds on which kumaras were grown.

TE AKAU : *te:* the; *akau:* rocky coast. The name was given by the tohunga (priest) of the Tainui canoe because it was too rough to land here.

TE AKO-O-TE-TUI-A-TAMAOHO : the teaching of Tamaoho's tui bird. It was by a waterfall on the Whangamarino Stream. Tuis were taught to speak, usually by a waterfall where there was no other sound to disturb the sound of the teacher's voice.

TE ANAHAWEA : *te:* the; *ana:* cave; *Hawea:* the Hawea tribe. Smoke was seen coming from this cave in Bligh Sound in 1842, but the inhabitants of the "lost tribe" fled. Subsequently this name was applied to the sound.

TE ANAHINATORE : *te:* the; *ana:* cave; *hinatore:* phosphorescent. This is the famous recently rediscovered glow-worm cave of Te Anau, named Te Ana-au.

TE ANAU : A much disputed name. The following are some of the explanations given: to move to and fro as reeds in a lake; named after a Waitaha chieftainess; the rain on the water; the uneven surface; the long view; the lake of many

arms; water current in a cave. It seems most likely that it was named after Te Anau, the daughter of Hekeia.

TE ANGA : *te:* the; *anga:* cockleshell, or fruit stone.

TE ARA-A-HONGI : Hongi's Track, q.v.

TE ARAI : *te:* the; *arai:* screen.

TE ARAROA : *te:* the; *ara:* path; *roa:* long. The long path. The name was given by the Maoris first to the residence of a missionary who had a long path to the front of his house.

TE ARAWHATA : the ladder or bridge. A ravine which gave access to the Panekiri Bluff, Waikaremoana.

TE ARO : *te:* the; *aro:* face, or front.

TE AROHA : *te:* the; *aroha:* love or affection. Kahumata-momoe sat on the summit of this mountain of love, and his heart was filled with affection for the land and people of Te Paeroa-o-Toi, the long range of Toi.

TE ATATU : *te:* the; *atatu:* dawn.

TE AU : the cloud or fog, the site of the Town Belt in Dunedin.

TE AUMITI : *te:* the; *au:* current; *miti:* swallowed up. The Maori name for French

Pass which in legend was formed by a cormorant.

TE AUNUIOTONGA : *te:* the; *au:* current; *nui:* great; *o:* of; *tonga:* south. The Manawatu Gorge through which the south winds blow.

TE AUTE : *te:* the; *aute:* paper mulberry tree. The name commemorates an unsuccessful attempt to grow this tropical tree, which is so important to the Polynesians.

TE AWA : *te:* the; *awa:* river, or channel.

TE AWAITI : *te:* the; *awa:* river, or channel; *iti:* little. The little channel.

TE AWAMUTU : *te:* the; *awa:* river; *mutu:* cut short, or ended. The river above this point was blocked by snags and unsuitable for canoes.

TE HANA : *te:* the; *hana:* glow.

TE HAPARA : *te:* the; *hapara:* spade.

TE HAROTO : *te:* the; *haroto:* pool.

TE HEUHEU : *te:* the; *heuheu:* brushwood. The body of a famous chief was buried near Lake Taupo, and it was difficult to find at a later date because of the brushwood that had grown over it. The high chief Tukino had a son who was named Te Heuheu from this event, and the highest peak of Mount Tongariro bears his name.

TE HINAU : *te:* the; *hinau:* native tree.

TE HOE : Short for Hoe-o-Tanui, q.v.

TE HOIERE : named after a canoe, it is the Maori name for Pelorus Sound.

TE HOPE : *te:* the; *hope:* waist. This river crossing was waist-deep.

TE HORO : *te:* the; *horo:* landslide. A descriptive name.

TE HURIA : *te:* the; *huria:* Maori form of Judea.

TE IKA-A-MAUI : *te:* the; *ika:* fish; *a:* of; *Maui:* the discoverer of New Zealand. The North Island was his fish which he pulled up from the depths of the ocean.

TE IKA-A-PAREHIKA : the fish of Parehika. The Maori name of Lawyers Head, Dunedin, which legend says was a fish which Parehika pulled from the sea.

TE IKA-A-POUTINI : the fish of Poutini. An ancient name for the West Coast. Traditionally greenstone was the fish of Poutini.

TE IKA-A-WHATAROA : *te:* the; *ika:* fish; *whata:* storehouse; *roa:* long. The long fish storehouse.

TE KAHA : *te:* the; *kaha:* rope, or boundary line.

TE KAIRANGA : the place where much food is gathered. Forest, river, and lagoon teemed with birds and fish, and the land was suitable for cultivation. The Maori name for Linton Military Camp.

TE KAKAHO : *te:* the; *kakaho:* toetoe or plume-grass.

TE KAKAPO : *te:* the; *kakapo:* ground parrot. Kahu's dog caught a kakapo here.

TE KAMINARU : Correctly Te Ika-a-Maru, the fish of Maru.

TE KAO : *te:* the; *kao:* dried kumara.

TEKAPO : Correctly Takapo; *taka:* a floor mat; *po:* night. An exploring party was surprised and frightened at night; they hastily rolled up their sleeping mats and took their departure.

TE KARAKA : *te:* the; *karaka:* native tree.

TE KAUANGA-A-HATU-PATU : *te:* the; *kauhanga:* swimming; *a:* of; *Hatupatu:* the young man of Rotorua who dived into the lake and swam underwater to Mokoia Island.

TE KAUKAROA : In full Te Kaukaharoa; *te:* the; *kaukaha:* to swim strongly; *roa:* long. The long, strong swimming of Hikaroa, who swam across Lake Te Anau at its widest part.

TE KAUWHATA : *te:* the; *kau:* empty; *whata:* storehouse.

TE KAWA : *te:* the; *kawa:* shrub.

TE KAWAKAWA : *te:* the; *kawakawa:* shrub. The daughters of Kupe made a wreath of the leaves of kawakawa, and this place later became Cape Palliser. Several places with this name were remembered as place names from Hawaiki.

TE KIRI : *te:* the; *kiri* (short for *kirikiri*) : gravel.

TE KITEROA : *te:* the; *kite:* to see; *roa:* long. The long view.

TE KOHAKA POUAKAI : *te:* the; *kohaka* (South Island form of *kohanga*) : nest; *pouakai:* fabulous gigantic bird.

TE KOHANGA : *te:* the; *kohanga:* nest.

TE KOPI : *te:* the; *kopi:* meeting of streams.

TE KOPURU : *te:* the; *kopuru:* heavy clouds.

TE KOROA : *te:* the; *koroa:* finger.

TE KOURA : *te:* the; *koura:* crayfish.

TE KOWHAI : *te:* the; *kowhai:* flowering tree.

TE KUITI : A contraction of Te Kuititanga, the narrowing in. A reference to the confiscation of Maori property after the Waikato War, and also to the constriction of the valley of the Mangaokewa at this point.

TE KUMARA : *te:* the; *kumara:* sweet potato. The site of old kumara plantations.

TE KUMI : *te:* the; *kumi:* fabulous creature or monster.

TE KUPENGA-A-TARA-MAINUKU: *te:* the; *kupenga:* fishing net; *a:* of; *Taramainuku:* a chief. Taramainuku cast his net across the Hauraki Gulf from Cape Colville to Whangarei Heads. The Watchman was the centre post of the net, and the Hen and Chicken Islands the corks.

TE KUPENGA-O-KUPE : *te:* the; *kupenga:* fishing net; *o:* of; *Kupe:* the great explorer.

TE KURAE-O-TURA : the headland of Tura, the Maori name for the Devonport foreshore.

TE KURAETANGA-O-TE-IHU-O-HEI : *te:* the; *kuraetanga:* outward curve; *o:* of; *te:* the; *ihu:* nose; *o:* of; *Hei:* an explorer. The outward curve of Hei's nose, named by Hei as the Arawa canoe passed north to Hauraki. The island is sometimes known as The Chief's Nose.

TE KURI-A-PAWA : *te:* the; *kuri:* dog; *a:* of; *Pawa:* a famous Maori chief. Later re-named Young Nick's Head by Captain Cook.

TE MAHIA : *te:* the; *mahia:* indistinct sound.

TE MAIKA : *te:* the; *maika:* basket of cooked food.

TE MAIRE: *te:* the; *maire:* native tree.

TE MANIA : *te:* the; *mania:* plain.

TE MAPARA : *te:* the; *mapara:* resin, or comb.

TE MATA : *te:* the; *mata:* headland (and many other meanings).

TE MATAI: *te:* the; *matai:* native tree.

TE MATAU-A-MAUI : the fishhook of Maui, with which the fish of the North Island was hooked. The fishhook is the great curve of Hawke Bay.

TE MAUNGA : *te:* the; *maunga:* mountain.

TE MAUNGAROA : *te:* the; *maunga:* mountain; *roa:* long.

TE MAWHAI : *te:* the; *mawhai:* parasitic plant.

TE MIRA : *te:* the; *mira:* Maori form of mill. A flour mill once stood here.

TE MIRO : *te:* the; *miro:* native tree.

TE MOTU-TAPU-A-TIN-IRAU : *te:* the; *motu:* island; *tapu:* sacred; *a:* of; *Tinirau:* a legendary chief. The sacred island of Tinirau. An ancient name for Mokoia Island.

TEMUKA : Properly Te-umu-kaha; *te:* the; *umu:* oven; *kaha:* strong. The fierce oven. Another meaning given to the name is Strong current, *umu* here meaning current.

TE NAMU : *te:* the; *namu:* sandfly. Such names were usually given because of the presence of sandflies.

TE NGAE : *te:* the; *ngae:* swamp.

TENGAWAI : Probably a corruption of Te Anawai; *te:* the; *ana:* cave; *wai:* water. The water cavern.

TE NGAWHA : *te:* the; *ngawha:* sulphurous springs. A descriptive name.

TE NGUTU - O - TE - MANU : *te:* the; *ngutu:* beak; *o:* of; *te:* the; *manu:* bird. The beak of the bird.

TE NIHO-O-TE-KIORE : *te:* the; *niho:* tooth; *o:* of; *te:* the; *kiore:* rats. Rats' teeth. From an expression of Ihenga's wife when he brought home a bundle of rats and she saw their teeth.

TE PAHU : *te:* the; *pahu:* gong (a stone or piece of wood which was struck to summon the people).

TE PAKI : *te:* the; *paki:* fine weather, and other meanings.

TE PAPA : *te:* the; *papa:* flat land. A descriptive name.

TE PAPAPA : *te:* the; *papapa:* calabash. At one time known locally as Pumpkin Flat, which could be said to be a rough translation of the name.

TE PAPATAPU : *te:* the; *papa:* flat; *tapu:* sacred. The sacred flat.

TE PARI : *te:* the; *pari:* precipice, a descriptive name for Sheerdown Mountain, Milford Sound.

TEPENE : Maori form of the name of a missionary, Stephenson.

TE PIRITA: *te:* the; *pirita:* supplejack.

TE POHUE : *te:* the; *pohue:* climbing plant such as convolvulus, clematis, etc.

TE POI : *te:* the; *poi:* ball.

TE POKOHIWI : *te:* the;

Poi: flax ball

pokohiwi: shoulder. The Maori name for Boulder Bank.

TE PUAPUA - O - HINE - NUI-TE-PO : the entrance to the goddess of death. The fumerole which is now known as the Brain Pot at Whakarewarewa.

TE PUIA : geyser or hot spring.

TE PUKA-A-MAUI : *te:* the; *puka* (South Island form of *punga*) : anchor stone; *a:* of; *Maui:* the explorer. The Maori name for Stewart Island.

TE PUKE : *te:* the; *puke:* hill.

TE PUNA : *te:* the; *puna:* spring.

TE PUNA-A-TUHOE : the springs of Tuhoe, the Maori name for Fairy Springs.

TE PUNINGA : *te:* the; *puninga:* camping place.

TE PUROTU : handsome. One old chief said to another, "Te purotu o te wahine!" (What a beautiful wife you have!) and from this circumstance the place received its name.

TE RA : *te:* the; *ra:* sun. The Maori name for Daggs Sound, which opens up well to the sun.

TERAPATIKI : *tera:* that; *patiki:* flounder (fish).

TE RANGA-O-TAIKEHU: *te:* the; *ranga:* sandspit; *o:* of;

Taikehu: a member of the crew of Tainui who swam from this sandspit to the shore at Devonport. A fishing bank is also similarly named.

TE RAUAMOA : Probably Te Rauhamoa. *te:* the; *rauhamoa:* extinct bird.

TE RAWA : *te:* the; *rawa:* property, or the cause of a quarrel.

TERAWHITI : Properly Tarawhiti : near to the sunrise, or disturbed crossing.

TE REINGA : the leaping place of spirits. Wairua (souls) lowered themselves from a branch of a pohutukawa at Te Reinga into the underworld below the kelp.

TE RERE : *te:* the; *rere:* leap. *Rere, rerenga,* and *rereka,* all with the same meaning, are

Te Reinga: departing place of spirits

components of many place names, often recording some famous leap such as that of Hihi who leaped hundreds of feet to escape his enemies. His fall was broken by trees, and the place named Te Rere-a-Hihi.

TE RERENGAWAIRUA: *te:* the; *rerenga:* leaping; *wairua:* soul. The leaping place of souls. See also Te Reinga.

TE REREWA: *te:* the; *rerewa:* Maori form of devil. A name given to a supposedly wicked man by missionary Maoris.

TE RORE: *te:* the; *rore:* snare.

TE ROTO: *te:* the; *roto:* lake. A component of many names.

TE ROU: *te:* the; *rou:* fowler. The name given because the postmaster was called Fowler.

TE RUA: *te:* the; *rua:* pit. A component of several names.

TE RUAHINE: *te:* the; *ruahine:* old, or wise woman.

TE TAO-O-KUPE: the spear of Kupe. The Maori name for Jackson's Head where Kupe attempted to cast a spear across Cook Strait.

TE TATUA: *te:* the; *tatua:* girdle. Maori name for Three Kings, Auckland.

TE TAUMANU-O-TE-WAKA-A-MAUI: the thwart of Maui's canoe at Kaikoura.

TE TAUMATA: See under Taumata.

TE TAWA: *te:* the; *tawa:* native tree. At Te Tawa, Rotorua, Ihenga pushed his canoe with a piece of tawa wood. It stuck in the ground and he left it there, naming the place after it.

TE TEKO: *te:* the; *teko:* rock.

TE TI: *te:* the; *ti:* cabbage tree.

TE TIPUA: *te:* the; *tipua:* goblin.

TE TO: *te:* the; *to:* hauling up place. The Maori name for Freeman's Bay, Auckland.

TE TOU-O-TE-MA-TENGA: the sitting place of Marsden. A place where the Rev. Samuel Marsden sat to talk to the Maoris.

TE TUA: *te:* the; *tua:* other side, or days gone by.

TE TUAHU-A-TUA-MEKE-TE-AHI-TAPOA-I-TAONA-AI-TE-MANAWA-O-TAIAPUA: the sacred place of Tuameke, the fire of witchcraft incantation in which the heart of Taiapua was cooked. Between the Green and Blue Lakes, Rotorua.

TE UKU: *te:* the; *uku:* white clay.

TE UMU: *te:* the; *umu:*

oven. A component of many place names.

TE WAEWAE: *te:* the; *waewae:* leg, foot, or footprint.

TEWAHI: *te:* the; *wahi:* place. A component of several names.

TE WAI: *te:* the; *wai:* water, or stream. A common component of place names, usually followed by a personal name, or name of a plant or tree.

TE WAI POUNAMU: an old name for the South Island, The water of greenstone. It should really be Te Wahi pounamu, the place of greenstone.

TE WAITERE; *te:* the; *wai:* water; *tere:* swiftly flowing. The place was named in 1905, partly because of its meaning and partly in memory of the Rev. John Whiteley, as it is the Maori pronunciation of his name.

TE WAKA-A-MAUI: the canoe of Maui, from which he fished up the North Island. An old name for the South Island.

TE WEKA: *te:* the; *weka:* woodhen.

TE WERA: *te:* the; *wera:* heat, or burning.

TE WETA: *te:* the; *weta:* large native insect.

TE WHAITI: *te:* the; *whaiti:* narrow gorge. The full name is Te Whaiti-nui-a-Toi, the great canyon of Toi.

TE WHAKARAUPO: *te:* the; *whaka* (South Island form of *whanga*): harbour; *raupo:* reed. Harbour of the raupo reed, the Maori name for Lyttelton Harbour.

TE WHANGANUI-A-TARA: *te:* the; *whanganui:* great harbour; *a:* of; *Tara:* ancestor of the Ngai-Tara. The great harbour of Tara, now Wellington Harbour or Port Nicholson. However, it seems more likely that the meaning was The great waiting of Tara, who waited to take revenge on enemies who had killed and eaten his dog.

TE WHATA: *te:* the; *whata:* food storehouse. Ihenga raised a foodstore there.

Tiki: grotesque carved figure

TE WHETU: *te:* the; *whetu:* star.

TIHAKA: a kind of basket.

TIKINUI: *tiki:* carved figure in wood or greenstone; *nui:* big. Large tiki.

TIKITAPU: *tiki:* image; *tapu:* sacred. A young woman lost a greenstone tiki while she was bathing in the lake. The Maori name for the Blue Lake.

TIKITERE: a contraction of Taku tiki i tere nei, My youngest daughter has floated away. The young woman jumped into a boiling pool. Tiki is an endearing contraction of *potiki,* last-born.

TIKITIKI: girdle, or knot of hair.

TIKOKINO: *tiko:* evacuation; *kino:* bad.

TIKORANGI: *tiko:* to protrude; *rangi:* sky. The true Maori name which means Sky-piercer.

TIKORAUROHE: the latrine in the bracken fern.

TIMARU: *ti:* cabbage tree; *maru:* shelter. The true name is probably Te Maru, the place of shelter.

TIMATANGA: the beginning, or starting point.

TINAARUHE: *tina:* fixed; *aruhe:* fern-root. To be prevented from eating fern-root.

TINAKORI: Correctly Tinakore: *tina:* Maori form of the word dinner; *kore:* none. No dinner. Maori workmen on the road forgot to take their dinners with them. The hill (properly Otari) may have been named after the road.

TINIROTO: *tini:* many; *roto:* lakes. Many lakes. A modern descriptive name.

TINOPAI: *tino:* very; *pai:* good.

TINUI: *ti:* cabbage tree; *nui:* many. Many cabbage trees, a descriptive name.

TIORI-PATEA: *tiori:* to hold up to view; *patea:* clear. The Maori name for the Haast Pass. A leader of a group of travellers called out that the path was clear.

TIPAPA: *ti:* cabbage tree; *papa:* flat. Cabbage tree flat.

Ti: cabbage tree

117

TIRAORA : *tira:* a company of travellers; *ora:* satisfied. The original name of the bay was Tira, but ora was added to distinguish it from Tirau.

TIRATU : mast of a canoe.

TIRAU : *ti:* cabbage tree; *rau:* many. Many cabbage trees.

TIRAUMEA : many waving cabbage trees.

TIRITIRI : In full, Tiritiri-matangi; *tiritiri:* a twig which indicates the position of a kumara tuber; *matangi:* the warm north-east breeze.

TIROHANGA : view.

TIROHIA : look, or behold.

TIROITI : circumscribed view.

TIROMOANA : *tiro:* view; *moana:* ocean. Sea view.

TIRONUI : *tiro:* view; *nui:* great. Great view.

TIROPAHI : *tiro:* view; *pahi:* a large sea-going canoe with sails. View of a large canoe.

TIROROA : *tiro:* view; *roa:* long. Extensive view.

TITAHI : *ti:* cabbage tree; *tahi:* single. A single cabbage tree.

TITI : mutton bird.

TITIRANGI : *titi:* long streaks of cloud; *rangi:* sky. Long streaks of cloud in the sky. Or *titirangi:* a species of veronica.

TITIROA : very long streaks of cloud.

TITITEA : *titi:* peak; *tea:* white. Steep peak of glistening white. The Maori name for Mount Aspiring.

TITOKI : a native tree.

TITRI : A corruption of the Pakeha name tea-tree (for manuka).

TOA : male, brave, or warrior.

TOATOA : a native tree.

TOETOES : named after a Maori, Totoe.

TOKA : rock.

TOKAANU : *toka:* stone; *anu:* cold. A cold stone.

TOKAKARORO : *toka:* rock; *karoro:* sea-gull. Sea-gull rock.

Toa: warrior

TOKANUI : *toka:* rock; *nui:* many. Plenty of rocks.

TOKARAHI : *toka:* rock; *rahi:* many. Many rocks, because of the many blocks of limestone.

TOKAROA : *toka:* rock; *roa:* long. Long rock.

TOKATOKA : rocks upon rocks. A descriptive name for the lava crag above Wairoa.

TOKERAU : Properly Tokarau; *toka:* rocks; *rau:* hundred, or many. A hundred rocks. The Maori name for the Bay of Islands.

TOKIRIMA : *toki:* adze; *rima:* five. Five adzes.

TOKO : pole, or to propel.

TOKOITI : *toko:* pole; *iti:* small. Little poles. Or possibly Tokaiti, little rocks.

TOKOMARU : the canoe which brought Manaia to New Zealand. Literally, *toko:* staff; *maru:* shade or shelter.

TOKOROA : *toko:* pole; *roa:* long. Long pole.

TOKOTEA : Correctly Tokatea; *toka:* stone; *tea:* white. White rock. Kahu-mata-momoe placed a white rock on a hill in memory of his father Tama-te-kapua.

TOLAGA : An obvious corruption of a Maori name. One conjecture is that when Captain Cook recorded the name he pointed north-west to the mainland and asked what the place was called. The Maoris may have thought he was asking the name of the wind, and replied Tarakaka, south-west wind. The original name of Tolaga Bay was Uawa.

TOMOANA: named after a chief. Literally, *to:* to drag; *moana:* ocean.

TONGAPORUTU : *tonga:* south wind; *po:* night; *rutu:* to drive into. Driving into a southerly at night. Whatonga's canoe Kurahaupo was running down the west coast when it struck a southerly here at nightfall.

TONGARIRO : *tonga:* south wind; *riro:* carried away. When Ngatoro-i-rangi was on the summit and in danger of perishing with cold, he called to his sisters in Hawaiki for fire. His words were carried on the wings of the south wind. This name was originally applied to the three peaks, Tongariro, Ngauruhoe, and Ruapehu.

TOPUNI : close together, or a black dogskin cloak.

TOREA : oyster-catcher.

TORERE : named after a woman who swam ashore from the Tainui canoe. Literally, to hurry, or fall headlong.

TOTARA : a native tree. Totara in North Otago was so

named because it was the only one of its kind in that district. At one time this place was called Totaratahi, a single totara.

TOTARANUI : *totara:* tree; *nui:* many. Many totaras.

TOWAI : a native tree.

TUAHIWI : *tua:* on the other side; *hiwi:* ridge. On the other side of the ridge.

TUAI : dark.

TUAKAU : *tu:* to stand; *akau:* shore or coast. To stand by the shore of the river. There was a commanding view down the Waikato for some miles from this place.

TUAMARINA : Correctly Tuamarino; *tua:* beyond; *marino:* calm. Clear view from the plains to the hills.

TUAPEKA : *tua:* beyond; *peka:* branch of a river. On the further side of the stream.

TUATAPERE : a sacred ceremony before a time for amusement. There has been a suggestion that the name should be Tuatapera, pout of the lips, because of water being bitter.

TUATARA : native reptile.

TUHAWAIKI : named after a famous Maori chief of Otago, known as Bloody Jack.

TUHUA : obsidian. Also the Maori name for Mayor Island, named by Toi. It is an extinct volcano and there are large deposits of obsidian.

TUI : native bird.

TUKITUKI : to demolish, or batter. See under Ruatahuna.

TUMAHU : *tu:* wounded; *mahu:* healed. Healed of a wound.

TUMAI : *tu:* to stand; *mai:* this way, or towards the person speaking.

TUMOANA : *tu:* to stand; *moana:* ocean, or lake. Standing in the lake.

TUNA : eel.

TUNANUI : *tuna:* eel; *nui:* many. Plenty of eels.

TUPAROA: *tupa:* shellfish; *roa:* long. Long shellfish.

TURAKINA : to be felled or thrown down. Hau, when pursuing his wife, named the stream because a tree was lying across it.

TURANGA : standing. It was a stopping place of Toi's canoe, and was the site of the modern Gisborne. It was also known as Turanga-nui-a-Kiwa. Turanga-a-Kupe was the stopping place of Kupe, and is now Seatoun in Wellington.

TURANGARERE : Correctly Turanga-a-rere. *turanga:* standing; *a:* of; *rere:* to fly or wave. It was a place where a *taua* (war party) stood with feathers waving in their hair.

TURANGI : named after a chief. Literally, *tu:* to stand; *rangi:* sky. To stand in the sky.

TUREHU : fairies.

TURIROA : *turi:* post; *roa:* long. Long post.

TURUA : beautiful, referring to the reflections in the river.

TURUTURU-MOKAI : *turuturu:* to set a post in the ground; *mokai:* slave. A slave was captured on the spot where the post was set in.

TUTAEKURI : *tutae:* dung; *kuri:* dog.

TUTAENUI : *tutae:* dung; *nui:* big. The Maori name for Marton.

TUTAMOE : *tu:* to rise up; *tamoe:* flat top. Mountain rising up with a flat top.

TUTIRA : row, or file.

TUTOKO : named after a chief. Literally, *tu:* to stand; *toko:* post. To stand up like a post.

TUTUKAKA : *tutu:* a tree in which snares are set; *kaka:* parrot. The kaka perch.

TUTURAU : *tutu:* native tree; *rau:* many. Many tutu trees.

TUTUTAWA : *tutu:* to steep, in water; *tawa:* a native tree. The place where tawa berries are steeped in water.

UAWA : *ua:* rain; *wa:* season. Rainy season. The original name for Tolaga Bay, q.v.

UIA : to be disentangled.

UMERE : to keep in time by chanting.

UMUKURI : *umu:* oven; *kuri:* dog. Dog cooked in the oven. What was cooked in the oven was really Kurimanga, a *tohunga* (priest).

UMUTAOROA : *umu:* oven; *tao:* to cook; *roa:* long. The ovens that took a long time to cook. An incident in Maori history. The site of present day Dannevirke.

UMUTOI : *umu:* oven; *toi:* to be moist.

UMUWHEKE : *umu:* oven; *wheke:* octopus. Octopus cooked in an oven.

UPOKO-NGARO : *upoko:* head; *ngaro:* hidden. Hidden head. Ira-nga-rangi was desolate when her brothers were killed and she died of grief. Lest she should be mutilated by enemies, her people cut off her head and hid it in a cave by this stream.

UPOKO-POITO : *upoko:* head; *poito:* float. Heads like floats on a fishing net. Some Maoris were drowned here, and their heads bobbed up and down like floats on the water. This was near the foreshore at Napier.

UPOKORORO: a fresh-water fish.

URENUI: Manaia named the river after his son Tu-ure-nui. Literally, *ure:* figurative expression for courage; *nui:* big. Great courage.

UREWERA: The name was given almost sarcastically because a chief received a severe burn when he rolled into a fire during sleep.

URUPUKAPUKA: *uru:* grove; *pukapuka:* shrub. A grove of pukapukas.

URUTI: *uru:* grove; *ti:* cabbage tree. A grove of cabbage trees.

URUWHENUA: *uru:* west; *whenua:* land. West country.

UTIKU: a Biblical name, Eutychus, in its Maori form. The name was chosen by the chief Potaka when he came under missionary influence.

W

WAENGA: in the middle.

WAERENGA: a clearing.

WAERENGA-A-HIKA: *waerenga:* a clearing; *a:* of; *Hika:* name of a chief. Waerenga's clearing.

WAERENGA - O - KURI: *waerenga:* a clearing; *o:* of;

Waharoa: entrance to pa

Kuri: name of a chief. Kuri's clearing.

WAHAROA: *waha:* mouth; *roa:* long, i.e. the gateway to a palisaded village. Named after the great chief Te Waharoa.

WAIANAKARUA: *wai:* water; *ana:* cave; *rua:* two. Water from two caves, or the meeting of waters. Or else the creek of Nakarua.

WAIANIWA: Probably a contraction of Waianiwaniwa. *wai:* water; *aniwaniwa:* rain-bow. Deep water, or water in which the rainbow is reflected.

WAIANIWANIWA: *wai:* water; *aniwaniwa:* rainbow, or deep. Deep water, or water where rainbows appear in the spray.

WAIAPU: *wai:* water; *apu:* to swallow. Swallowing waters.

The river is dangerous to cross in time of flood. The rendering may be *waiapu:* a special kind of stone found only in this district, used for polishing adzes.

WAIAREKA: *wai:* water; *reka:* sweet. Sweet or pleasant water.

WAIARI: *wai:* water; *ari:* clear. Clear water.

WAIARIKI: hot springs, or curative waters. They are the *ariki:* chiefs or patriarchs of all water.

WAIARUHE: *wai:* water; *aruhe:* edible fernroot. Stream where the fernroot can be obtained.

WAIATARUA: *waiata:* song; *rua:* two. Two songs. Or *wai:* water; *atarua:* two images. Double-imaged water. The Maori name for Lake St. John, Auckland, now drained.

WAIAU: *wai:* water; *au:* current. River of swirling currents.

WAIAUA: *wai:* water; *aua:* native fish. Kahu-mata-momoe and Huarere saw the fish in the river and conferred the name.

WAIAUTOA: See Waiau-uha.

WAIAUUHA: *wai:* water; *au:* current; *uha:* female. The female Waiau. The male river was Waiautoa (Clarence River). Their sources are close to-

gether. In legend they were lovers who drifted apart, and weep for each other.

WAIAWA: *wai:* water; *awa:* valley. River in the valley.

WAIHAHA: *wai:* water; *haha:* noisy. Noisy water.

WAIHAO: *wai:* water; *hao:* a small eel. Eel river. The name is common. The South Canterbury river was named and discovered by a chief whose wife found these eels particularly acceptable.

WAIHAPA: *wai:* water; *hapa:* crooked. Crooked stream.

WAIHARAKEKE: *wai:* water; *harakeke:* flax. Water where the flax grows. At Blenheim the Maori name has been changed to the English equivalent Flaxbourne.

WAIHARARA: *waiha:* variety of kumara; *rara:* there.

WAIHARURU: *wai:* water; *haruru:* resounding. Rumbling or resounding water, descriptive of the sulphur area at Whakarewarewa.

WAIHAU: *wai:* water; *hau:* wind. Windy water.

WAIHEKE: *wai:* water; *heke:* to ebb or drip. Ebbing water.

WAIHEMO: *wai:* water; *hemo:* to disappear. Disappearing water, referring to the

the river when the tide has gone out.

WAIHI : *wai:* water; *hi:* gushing forth. Water gushing out. An old Hawaiki name.

WAIHIHI : gushing water, a name which comes from Hawaiki.

WAIHINAU : *wai:* water; *hinau:* native tree. Hinau trees by the water.

WAIHIRERE : *wai:* water; *hirere:* to rush. Rushing waters.

WAIHO : Correctly Waiau, q.v.

WAIHOAKA : *wai:* water; *hoaka* (South Island form of *hoanga*) : sandstone. Sandstone stream.

WAIHOLA : *wai:* water; *hola* (a rendering of *hora*) : spread out. Spreading waters. It is a wide shallow lake.

WAIHOPAI : It should probably be Waiopai, The water of Pai.

WAIHOPO : *wai:* water; *hopo:* to be apprehensive. River that one fears to cross.

WAIHORA : *wai:* water; *hora:* spread out. Wide expanse of water. (Lake Ellesmere.)

WAIHOU : *wai:* water; *hou:* cold, or new. New or cold river. Probably New river, in the sense that it has cut a new channel.

WAIHUA : *wai:* water;

hua: fish roe. So named by a Maori because his dog ate a porcupine fish there, but left the roe.

WAI-ITI : *wai:* water; *iti:* little. Little river. A descriptive name.

WAIKAIA : Properly Waikea or Waikeha. *wai:* water; *keha:* burr. The stream where the *keha* grew. It was named by Rakaihautu because the native burr infested the place.

WAIKAKA : Short for Waikakahi. *wai:* water; *kakahi:* shellfish. Water where the shellfish may be found.

WAIKAKAHO : *wai:* water; *kakaho:* plumes of the toetoe. Toetoe plume water.

WAIKANA : Short for Waikanakana. *wai:* water; *kanakana:* lamprey. Lamprey river.

WAIKANAE : *wai:* water; *kanae:* mullet. Hau, who was searching for his wife, looked about out of the corner of his eye . . . ka ngahae nga pi, and likened his eyes to the glistening of the mullet.

WAIKARAKA: *wai:* water; *karaka:* native tree. Karaka river.

WAIKARE : *wai:* water; *kare:* to ripple. Rippling water.

WAIKAREITI : *wai:* water; *kare:* to ripple; *iti:*

little. See Waikaremoana.

WAIKAREMOANA : *wai:* water; *kare:* to ripple; *moana:* lake. Popularly rendered The sea of rippling waters, but it would be better as The sea of dashing waters, because the waves were agitated by the *taniwha* who formed the Wai-kare-taheke, the raging torrent that runs out of the lake.

WAIKARETU : *wai:* water; *karetu:* sweet-scented grass. Karetu river.

WAIKARI: ditch or trench. Of Waikari in Hawke's Bay Paoa's dog Whakao dug (*kari* meaning to dig) until he found water.

WAIKATO : *wai:* water; *kato:* to flow. Full flowing river.

WAIKAUKAU : *wai:* water; *kaukau:* to bathe. Bathing place.

WAIKAURA : *wai:* water; *kaura* (a form of *koura*) : crayfish. Crayfish were plentiful in this stream.

WAIKAWA : *wai:* water; *kawa:* bitter. Bitter water.

WAIKAWAU : *wai:* water; *kawau:* shag. Shag river.

WAIKERERU: *wai:* water; *kereru:* wood-pigeon. Kereru water.

WAIKERIA : *wai:* water; *keria:* dug out. A gouged out watercourse.

WAIKERIKERI : *wai:* water; *kerikeri:* rushing along violently. The Maori name for the Selwyn River.

WAIKEWAI : Properly Waikekewai; *wai:* water; *kekewai:* small dragonfly. Dragonfly stream.

WAIKIEKIE : *wai:* water; *kiekie:* climbing plant. Kiekie water.

WAIKIMIHIA : *wai:* water; *kimihia:* sought for; The sought for water, the Maori name for Hinemoa's Bath on Mokoia Island, to which Hinemoa swam from the mainland and in which she bathed on her arrival.

WAIKINO : *wai:* water; *kino:* bad. Unpleasant water.

WAIKITE : *wai:* water; *kite:* to see. This was a once-famous geyser at Whakare-warewa which could be seen clearly from Rotorua.

WAIKIWI : *wai:* water; *kiwi:* flightless bird. Kiwi stream.

WAIKOAU : *wai:* water; *koau:* shag. Shag river.

WAIKOHU : mist or fog.

WAIKOIKOI : *wai:* water; *koikoi:* cool. Cool water.

WAIKOKOPU : *wai·* water; *kokopu:* freshwater fish. Kokopu stream.

WAIKOKOWAI : *wai:* water; *kokowai:* red ochre.

Water where red ochre is found.

WAIKOMITI: *wai:* water; *komiti:* mingled. Mingled waters. The Maori name for Glen Eden.

WAIKOPUA: *wai:* water; *kopua:* deep, Deep water.

WAIKOROHIHI: bubbling or hissing water, a pool at Whakarewarewa.

WAIKOTUTURI: *wai:* water; *kotuturi:* kneeling. The water of kneeling. Some defeated warriors were forced to kneel beside the stream with their hands tied behind their backs.

WAIKOUAITI: *wai:* water; *koua (kua):* to become; *iti:* small. The water that decreased. The usual explanation of this name is that the river changed its course, the flow thus decreasing at this point.

WAIKOURA: *wai:* water; *koura:* crayfish. Crayfish stream.

WAIKOWHAI: *wai:* water;

Kumete: wooden bowl

kowhai: flowering tree. Many kowhais grew here.

WAIKUMETE: *wai:* water; *kumete:* wooden bowl. Kumete creek.

WAIKUTA: *wai:* water; *kuta:* a rush. Stream of rushes. The name was given by Ihenga because of the profuse growth of rushes.

WAIMA: *wai:* water; *ma:* white. White river. There was a great deal of white limestone in its bed.

WAIMAERO: *wai:* water; *maero:* wild man of the forest. The name is also said to mean deep water channel, or hard water.

WAIMAHAKA: *wai:* water; *mahaka* (South Island form of *mahanga*): twin. Twin waters.

WAIMAHORA: *wai:* water; *mahora:* to spread out. Spreading waters.

WAIMAHURU: *wai:* water; *mahuru:* placid. Placid waters. The name was given by Paoa because of the appearance of the stream.

WAIMAI: Probably the original name was Waimatai; *wai:* water; *matai:* black pine. Black pine river.

WAIMAKARIRI: *wai:* water; *makariri:* cold. Cold river.

WAIMAMAKU: *wai:*

water: *mamaku:* tree-fern. Mamaku stream.

WAIMANA : *wai:* water; *mana:* shrimp. Stream in which shrimps are caught.

WAIMANARARA : *wai:* water; *manarara:* noisy. Turbulent river.

WAIMANGAROA : *wai:* water; *manga:* branch; *roa:* long. Long branch of a river.

WAIMANGEO : *wai:* water; *mangeo:* pungent, mineralised water. The Maori name for Alum Creek.

WAIMANGU : *wai:* water; *mangu:* black. Black water. The name of the famous extinct geyser which threw up a huge volume of muddy water high into the air.

WAIMANU : *wai:* water; *manu:* bird. Stream frequented by birds.

WAIMARAMA : *wai:* water; *marama:* moonlight. Moonlit water. It also means clear water.

WAIMARIE : *wai:* water; *marie:* quiet. Quiet waters.

WAIMARINO : *wai:* water; *marino:* calm, or still. Still waters.

WAIMARU : *wai:* water; *maru:* sheltered. Calm water.

WAIMATA : *wai:* water; *mata:* bullet. Stream where bullets are found. A running fight took place there nearly a hundred years ago, and it is said that bullets may be found in the bed of the stream.

WAIMATAITAI : *wai:* water; *mataitai:* salty. Brackish water. A descriptive name of a lagoon.

WAIMATE : *wai:* water; *mate:* stagnant. The orignal name in the South Island was Waimatemate, with the same meaning. Until floods came, the creeks became blocked up and there were many stagnant pools.

WAIMATENUI : *wai:* water; *mate:* stagnant; *nui:* big. Great expanse of stagnant water.

WAIMATUKU : *wai:* water; *matuku:* bittern. Bittern stream.

WAIMAUKU : *wai:* water; *mauku:* small fern. A river which when flooded drowned the cabbage trees, so that their tops appeared above the water like small ferns.

WAIMAUNGA : *wai:* water; *maunga:* mountain. Mountain stream.

WAIMEA : Several meanings have been given to the name; *wai:* water; *mea:* unimportant, forgotten. The stream with the forgotten name. *Mea* may be a contraction of *meha:* tasteless. The use of the name is widespread, and could mean insipid, tasteless, unimportant, lonely, unpalatable, etc.

WAIMEHA: See Waimea.

WAIMIHA: Probably another form of Waimea, q.v. It may mean Water that is pretty to look at.

WAIMIHI: *wai:* water; *mihi:* to sigh, or regret.

WAIMIRO: *wai:* water; *miro:* native tree. Miro creek.

WAIMOARI: *wai:* water; *moari:* giant swing. The river beside which a moari was erected.

WAIMORI: *wai:* water; *mori:* without tributaries.

WAIMOTU: *wai:* water; *motu:* island. Island stream, or stream with an island in it.

WAINAMU: *wai:* water;

Moari: giant stride

namu: sandfly. Stream infested with sandflies.

WAINGARO: *wai:* water; *ngaro:* lost. Hidden waters.

WAINGAWA: Correctly Wai-a-wanga, water of hesitation. Hau hesitated to cross this river when in pursuit of his wife.

WAINGONGORO: *wai:* water; *ngongoro:* gurgling. It also means snoring, and this is the place where Turi snored.

WAINIHINIHI: *wai:* water; *nihinihi:* to glide past. The place where the waters glide past.

WAINUI: *wai:* water; *nui:* big. Big river.

WAINUIOMATA: *wai:* water; *nui:* big; *o:* of; *Mata:* name of a person. Big stream belonging to Mata.

WAIOEKA: Probably Waioweka; *wai:* water; *o:* of; *weka:* woodhen. Weka river.

WAIOMATATINI: The syllables are capable of so many meaningless translations that speculation is idle. It is the place where an ancestor of the Ngati-Porou tribe was hung up in a puriri tree, the incident being remembered by the giving of the famous name Tuwhakairiora.

WAINONO: *wai:* water; *nono:* oozing. Oozing water.

WAIOMU: *wai:* water; *o:*

of; *Mu:* personal name. The water of Mu.

WAIONE: *wai:* water; *one:* beach. Stream on the beach.

WAIONGONA : *wai:* water; *o:* of; *Ngona:* personal name. Water of Ngona.

WAIOPANI : *wai:* water; *o:* of; *pani:* orphan. Orphan water or lake.

WAIORAATANE : *wai:* water; *ora:* living; *a:* of; *Tane:* the god of nature. A very famous name in mythology.

WAIORONGOMAI : *wai:* water; *o:* of; *Rongomai:* personal name. The water of Rongomai.

WAIOTAPU : Sacred waters.

WAIOTEMARAMA : *wai:* water; *o:* of; *te:* the; *marama:* moon. The waters of the moon.

WAIOTIRA : *wai:* water; *o:* of; *tira:* sticks set up for purposes of divination. Water of incantation.

WAIOTU : *wai:* water; *o:* of; *Tu:* the god of war. A pool or stream where ceremonies were rendered to Tu.

WAIOURU : *wai:* water; *o:* of; *uru:* west. River of the west. The stream is the most westerly branch of the Hautupu River.

WAIPA : *wai:* water; *pa:* fortified village. River by the pa.

WAIPAHI : *wai:* water; *pahi:* flowing. Flowing water. Actually The water of Pahi.

WAIPANGO : *wai:* water; *pango:* black. Black water.

WAIPAO : *wai:* water; *pao:* to strike. The place was named after Waipao who was killed by Tuwhakairiora.

WAIAPAOA : *wai:* water; *paoa:* smoky. Smoky water. In actual fact it should be called Waiopaoa, the river of Paoa, a famous chief whose people had made a canoe in the forest. He created the river in order that the canoe could be launched.

WAIPAPA : *wai:* water; *papa:* flat, or flat rock. Stream across the plain, or stream of the flat rock.

WAIPAPAKAURI : *wai:* water; *papa:* flat land; *kauri:* native tree. Swampy ground where the kauri grows.

WAIPARA : *wai:* water; *para:* mud. River with a thick muddy sediment.

WAIPATA : *wai:* water; *pata:* dripping. Dripping water.

WAIPATIKI : *wai:* water; *patiki:* flounder. Water where the flounders may be found.

WAIPATUKAHU : *wai:* water; *patu:* to beat; *kahu:* cloak. Water in which garments were beaten.

WAIPAWA : *wai:* water; *pawa:* bird-snare. Waipawa in

Hawke's Bay is named after Pawa or Paoa, but has also been rendered Waipawamate, water smelling strongly, or dead water.

WAIPIATA : *wai:* water; *piata:* glistening. Glistening water.

WAIPIPI : *wai:* water; *pipi:* shellfish. Where the pipis are found.

WAIPIRO : *wai:* water; *piro:* stinking. Evil-smelling water.

WAIPORI : Correctly Waipouri; *wai:* water; *pouri:* dark. Dark river.

WAIPOUA : *wai:* water; *poua:* shellfish. The original name was probably Waipoa, *poa* being a shellfish found at the mouth of the river. Another conjecture is that the name is *wai:* water; *po:* night; *ua:* rain; water that comes from the rain at night.

WAIPOUNAMU : *wai:* water; *pounamu:* greenstone. Greenstone river.

WAIPOURI : *wai:* water; *pouri:* dark. Dark stream.

WAIPU : *wai:* water; *pu:* red. Reddish water. A fairly persistent belief is that *pu* refers to the sound of gunfire.

WAIPUKU : *wai:* water; *puku:* to swell. Swelling water.

WAIPUKURAU : *wai:* water; *pukurau:* a large white mushroom. Stream where the mushrooms grow. This is the correct meaning, but it has been conjectured that the name should have been Waipukerau; *waipuke:* flood; *rau:* many. Many floods.

WAIRAKEI : *wai:* water; *rakei:* adorning. The place where the pools were used as mirrors.

WAIRAKI : *wai:* water; *raki:* dry. Dried up waters. It is the bed of an old lake.

WAIRANGI : foolish, or excited.

WAIRARAPA : *wai:* water; *rarapa:* glistening. Glistening waters. When Hau saw the beautiful lake and valley his eyes glistened with delight. The glistening is not only of the water but of his eyes.

WAIRAU : *wai:* water; *rau:* many. The plain of a hundred rivers. Simple names like this often have many meanings, and some that have been given for Wairau are, The rift in the clouds, Waters of many streams, and Discoloured waters.

WAIREKA : *wai:* water; *reka:* sweet. Pleasant waters.

WAIREPO : *wai:* water; *repo:* swamp. Swampy water, or Water running through a swamp.

WAIRERE : waterfall.

WAIREWA : *wai:* water; *rewa:* to lift up. Water lifted up. It is the Maori name for Lake Forsyth, the last lake which Rakaihautu scooped out. As the sign that his labours were over, he thrust his *ko* (digging stick) into the summit of a hill close by, and this was the "lifting up".

WAIRIMA : *wai:* water; *rima:* five.

WAIRIO : *wai:* water; *rio:* dried up. Dried up waters. Another conjecture is that the name should be Waireo; *wai:* water; *reo:* voice. Voice of the waters.

WAIROA: *wai:* water; *roa:* long. Usually Long river, but in some places it means High waterfall, and in one case Tall geyser.

WAIRONGOA : *wai:* water; *rongoa:* medicine. Water with curative properties.

WAIRONGOMAI : Probably the correct form is Waiorongomai, the water of Rongomai.

WAIRUA : soul or spirit. Or *wai:* water; *rua:* two. Two streams.

WAIRUNA : *wai:* water; *runa:* dock plant. Stream where the dock grows.

WAIRUNGA : *wai:* water; *runga:* above, or from above.

Stream which flows from the mountains.

WAITAHA : *wai:* water; *taha:* to pass on one side. Backwater. Some South Island names come from the early Waitaha tribe. Also a name for the Canterbury Plains, an abbreviation of Nga Pakihi-whakateketeka-a-Waitaha, q.v.

WAITAHANUI : *wai:* water; *tahanui:* a variety of cabbage tree. Stream where the cabbage trees grow. Or Big backwater.

WAITAHORA: *wai:* water; *tahora:* spread out, or a small duck. Duck stream, or Spreading waters.

WAITAHUNA : *wai:* water; *tahuna:* sandbank. Usually translated Stream of many sandbanks. Actually it was named after a Ngai-Tahu chief.

WAITAI : *wai:* water; *tai:* tide. Tidal or brackish water.

WAITAKARO: *wai:* water; *takaro:* to play or wrestle. Stream running through a games area.

WAITAKARURU : *wai:* water; *takaruru:* stagnant. Stagnant water. One amusing meaning has been given : *wai:* water; *taka:* to fall; *ruru:* owl. Water that the morepork fell into.

WAITAKERE: *wai:* water;

takere: deep. Deep pools. Another meaning is Cascading waters. It is thought that the Auckland Waitakere may possibly be a corruption of Waitekauri, stream where the kauri grows; but it is almost certain that it was named after a chief who was murdered at the mouth of the stream.

The South Island Waitakere (the Nile River) was originally Ngawaitakerei, The waters of Takerei.

WAITAKI : *wai:* water; *taki:* (South Island form of *tangi*): sounding. Rumbling waters, coming from the sound of the river over the shingle beds. There is a legend that the river was formed by the tears of two brothers whose sister was drowned at the mouth of the river, and turned into a rock. The brothers were transformed into two hills near Ohou, and their tears form the river of weeping.

WAITANGI : *wai:* water; *tangi:* weeping, or sounding. Noisy or weeping waters.

WAITAPU : *wai:* water; *tapu:* sacred. Sacred water.

WAITARA : *wai:* water; *tara* (short for *taranga*): wide steps. River crossed with big steps. Turi forded it with great strides. Another explanation is that it simply means Mountain

stream (*tara:* peak), and another that a young man searched for his father by successive throwings of his dart; *whai:* to follow; *tara:* dart.

Waitara on the Mohaka River is so named because he took with him the bones of his slave to scrape and shape into spears *(tara)*.

WAITARERE : *wai:* water; *tarere:* to flow copiously. Running streams.

WAITARIA : *wai:* water; *taria:* to wait for. Water that has been waited for.

WAITATA : *wai:* water; *tata:* close. Nearby water.

WAITATI : the proper name is Waitete : *wai:* water; *tete:* blue duck. Water frequented by blue ducks.

WAITEMATA: *wai:* water; *te:* the; *mata* (short for *matatuhua*): obsidian. Water as smooth as the surface of obsidian. The accent should really be placed on the final syllable. It may be a coincidence that the name of the upper reaches of the harbour was Waitimata, *timata,* to begin, being a rock which was a tribal boundary.

WAITEMATAMATA : *wai:* water; *te:* the; *Matamata:* a taniwha who lived in the creek.

WAITEPEKA : *wai:* water;

te: the; *peka:* branch. Tributary of the river.

WAITETE: *wai:* water; *tete:* dripping. Water dripping from the ground.

WAITETI: *wai:* water; *te:* the; *ti:* cabbage tree. Cabbage tree stream.

WAITETUNA: *wai:* water; *te:* the; *tuna:* eel. Creek where the eels are caught.

WAITOA: *wai:* water; *toa:* rough. Rough water.

WAITOETOE: *wai:* water; *toetoe:* plume grass. Toetoe stream.

WAITOHI: There are three possible explanations for the original name for Picton. It may be a stream where the *waitohi* baptismal rite was performed. It may be, in full, Te Wera-o-Waitohi, the burning of Waitohi. Waitohi, the sister of Te Rauparaha, is reputed to have been burnt to death in a scrub fire; or it is the clearing burnt by Waitohi to make a plantation.

WAITOHU: *wai:* water; *tohu:* to point out. Water that showed the way to two fugitives who escaped to the hills.

WAITOMO: *wai:* water; *tomo:* shaft. Water entering the cave by means of long shafts.

WAITOTARA: *wai:* water; *totara:* native tree. River

Totara: New Zealand tree

where the totara trees were plentiful.

WAITOTO: *wai:* water; *toto:* blood. Probably the scene of a battle.

WAITUI: *wai:* water; *tui:* native bird. Tui bay or river.

WAITUNA: *wai:* water; *tuna:* eel. Eel stream. It is possible that Waituna West received its Maori name because of an orator who lived there. Some eels remain small and immature, and the Maori ideal of oratory was a flow of words of even length.

WAIUKU: *wai:* water; *uku:* white clay. A high-born girl came here to choose a husband. The first chief presented was good-looking, but did not impress the girl. His brother who was in the kumara plantation was hurriedly summoned, and scrubbed with white clay from the stream to make him presentable. The *uku* was known as Maori soap. The story has a happy ending, and the event is commemorated in the name Waiuku.

WAIUTA : *wai:* water. *uta:* inland. Inland water. Or to load a canoe on the river.

WAIWERA : *wai:* water; *wera:* hot. Hot water. The Auckland Waiwera is the site of hot springs. The Southern Waiwera is named after Waiwhero, a chief.

WAIWHERO : *wai:* water; *whero:* red. Red water.

WAIWHETU : *wai:* water; *whetu:* star. Star-reflecting water.

WAIWHIO : *wai:* water; *whio:* blue mountain duck, or whistling duck. Stream of the mountain duck.

WAKAMARINO : *waka* (South Island form of *whanga*): harbour; *marino:* peaceful. A peaceful bay.

WAKANUI : *waka:* canoe; *nui:* big. Large canoe.

WAKAPATU : Correctly Whakapatu, to strike, or to kill.

WAKAPUAKA : Correctly Whakapuaka, the name of Kupe's fishing ground in

Whio: blue duck

Tahiti, transferred to Nelson. Literally *waka:* canoe; *puaka:* dry twigs. The early settlers called it Hoke-poke.

WAKARARA : *waka:* canoe; *rara:* to be thrown broadside on. A canoe thrown on its beam ends.

WAKARI: Properly Whakaari, to show, or expose to view.

WAKATAHURI : *waka:* canoe; *tahuri:* overturned. The overturned canoe.

WAKATIPU : Short for Wakatipuwaimaori. Wakatipu is said to be Wakatipua, *waka:* trough; *tipua:* goblin or monster. The lake was the trough in which the tipua rests, his breathing causing the rise and fall of the lake waters. On the other hand the original form may be Whakatipu, which means to create or cause to grow, so named because the remnants of defeated tribes retired here to rear their families and build up their strength.

Wakatipu-waimaori means Fresh water Wakatipu, and Lake McKerrow is Wakatipu-waitai, Saltwater Wakatipu.

WAKATU : *waka:* canoe; *tu:* to pile up. The place where broken canoes were dumped. It is the old name for Nelson.

WANAKA : Possibly it should be Wananga : sacred knowledge. Another explanation is that it is Oanaka (which has much the same sound), *o:* the place of; *Anaka:* name of a person.

WANGAEHU : See Whangaehu.

WANGANUI : See Whanganui.

WANGAPEKA : *wanga* (properly *whanga*): harbour or valley; *peka:* edible fern-root. Valley of the fern-root.

WAOTU : In full, He Wao-tutahi-nga-rakau, the place of high trees standing by themselves.

WAREA : to be absorbed, or to be made unconscious. Possibly named after the wife of Manaia.

WAREPA : Correctly, Wharepa, fortified house.

WARO : a deep pit, or a recess in the rocks.

WEKA : woodhen.

WEKAKURA : *weka:* woodhen; *kura:* red. Reddish coloured weka.

WERAROA : *wera:* burnt; *roa:* long. Long burn, in preparation for a clearing.

WHAINGAROA : *whai:* stingray; *nga:* the; *roa:* long. The Maori name for Raglan Harbour.

WHAKAANGIANGI : to make thin.

WHAKAARI : to make visible. The Maori name for White Island as well as other places.

WHAKAHORO : to scatter, or to take to pieces.

WHAKAIRI : to hang up.

WHAKAKI : to fill. This referred to the lagoon which the Maoris liked to see at a high level for fishing and eeling.

WHAKAKITENGA : a place where an extensive view can be obtained.

WHAKAMAHI : made to work. The men were forced to work in the cultivations and were fed with human flesh. On their return they said, "We were made to work and the food was human flesh."

WHAKAMARAMA : to illuminate, or to explain.

WHAKAMARINO : to make peaceful.

WHAKAPARA : to make a clearing in the forest.

WHAKAPOUNGAKAU: *whakapou:* to establish firmly; *ngakau:* heart. The hills of heart's desire. Tanewhakarara went to hunt in these hills and did not return. His sisters named the range because of the longing their brother had for them, and before they returned to Hawaiki they made hot springs at Tikitere so that their brother could bathe there if he returned.

WHAKAREWA : to cause something to float.

WHAKAREWAREWA : The full name is Te Whaka-rewarewatanga-o-te-Ope-a-Wahiao, the uprising of the war party at Wahiao. A war party assembled at the geyser area and performed a war dance before going into action.

WHAKARONGO: to listen, or to inform.

WHAKATAKI : to go in search of, or to begin a speech.

WHAKATANE : to play the man. Wairaka, the daughter of the chief Toroa, jumped ashore from the Mataatua canoe when it was in difficulties, and took a line ashore. Her famous saying on this occasion was, "Me whakatane au i au" (I shall act like a man).

There are several variations of the story.

WHAKATETE : disputed ground. A recent name applied to the sacred places where gold prospectors in the Coromandel Peninsula were not permitted to dig.

WHAKATITI : a leaf used to let the spirit of a dying man escape.

WHAKATU : to stand up, or to make a speech.

WHAKATUTU : to place an object so that water falls on to it, to hold open a basket, or to fasten a net to a hoop.

WHANANAKI : *whana:* to rush; *naki:* steadily. A steady rush (of water).

WHANAWHANA : to bend backwards and forwards.

WHANGAEHU : *whanga:*

Whakatu: to make a speech

136

harbour; *ehu:* turbid. *Ehu* also means to bail out, and it is said that when Hau crossed this river, he had to bail out his canoe; or else that he splashed the water with the flat of his taiaha.

WHANGAKOKO : *whanga:* harbour; *koko:* a name for the tui. Tui harbour.

WHANGAMATA: *whanga:* harbour; *mata:* obsidian. Obsidian is washed ashore here from Mayor Island.

WHANGAMOA : *whanga:* harbour; *moa:* extinct giant bird. Moa haven.

WHANGAMOMONA : *whanga:* valley; *momona:* fat. Fertile valley. There is also a story that a man named Hoti waylaid travellers and killed and ate the plump ones.

WHANGANUI : *whanga:* harbour; *nui:* big. Great harbour. The pronunciation of Maoris of this district is rather different from those in other parts, especially because they substitute w for wh. For this reason the form Wanganui has become the accepted spelling.

WHANGANUI - O - HEI : the great bay of Hei. The Maori name for Mercury Harbour.

WHANGAPARA : *whanga:* harbour; *para:* sediment. Muddy harbour.

WHANGAPARAOA : *whanga:* harbour; *paraoa:* whale. Whale harbour. This is the place where canoes of the great migration landed. A whale was stranded on the beach and became an object of dispute between the men of the Tainui and Arawa canoes.

WHANGAPE : It is said that the name means Waiting for the inside of the paua. The name comes from the Society Islands.

WHANGAPIPIRO : evil-smelling place. This was the hot spring in which the bird-ogress who chased Hatupatu was killed.

WHANGAPOUA: *whanga:* harbour; *poua:* shellfish. Harbour of shellfish.

Paraoa: whale

WHANGARA : *whanga:* harbour; *ra:* sun. Sunny bay. The name was brought from Rarotonga.

WHANGARAE : *whanga:* harbour; *rae:* headland. The bay of many capes, the Maori name for Croixelles Harbour.

WHANGARATA : *whanga:* harbour; *rata:* native tree. Bay of rata trees.

WHANGAREI : *whanga:* harbour; *rei:* cherished possession. It probably means The waiting of Rei. A young woman Reipae from Waikato waited here for her lover, but grew tired and married another young man. Her sister Reitu married the rejected lover.

WHANGAROA : *whanga:* harbour; *roa:* long.

WHANGARURU: *whanga:* harbour; *ruru:* sheltered. Sheltered harbour.

WHANGATEAU: *whanga:* harbour; *te:* the; *au:* current. The harbour with the strong current.

WHANGATOETOE : *whanga:* harbour; *toetoe:* plume grass. Toetoe bay.

WHARENUI : a variety of flax.

WHARE : house. The name is usually given by the Pakeha, as in Whare Flat.

WHAREATEA : *whare:*

house; *atea:* space, or out of the way. A large house to accommodate everyone. Such a house stood here for the entertainment of guests long ago.

WHAREHINE : *whare:* house; *hine:* young woman. The house of girls.

WHAREHUNGA : *whare:* house; *hunga:* company of people. A large house in which to accommodate people.

WHAREHUIA : *whare:* house; *huia:* extinct bird. Home of the huia.

WHAREKOPAE : house with a door at the side (an unusual place for the door).

WHAREKURI : Properly Te Warokuri, the chasm of the dog.

WHAREMA: *whare:* house. *ma:* free from tapu. Common house.

WHAREMAUKU : *whare:* house; *mauku:* fern. House built of fern-trees.

WHAREORINO : *whare:* house; *o:* of; *rino:* iron. Corrugated iron house.

WHAREPAINA : *whare:* house; *paina:* to warm oneself. It has been suggested that as it is in a region of pine plantations, *paina* stands for pine. The house in the pines.

WHAREPAPA : *whare:* house; *papa:* flat land. House on the flat.

WHAREPOA :   *whare:* house; *poa:* sacred food. House of sacred food.

WHAREPONGA :   *whare:* house; *ponga:* tree-fern. Tree-fern house.

WHARERAKAU :   *whare:* house; *rakau:* timber, or tree. House of timber, or house among the trees.

WHARERATA :   *whare:* house; *rata:* native tree. House among the ratas.

WHAREROA :   *whare:* house; *roa:* long. Long house.

WHARETOA :   *whare:* house; *toa:* warriors. House of men.

WHARETOTARA : whare: house; *totara:* native tree. The house made of totara bark.

WHARETUKURA: *whare:* house; *tukura:* a species of fern-tree. Fern-tree house.

WHATAARAMA : *whata:* food store; *a:* of; *Rama:* name of a man. The food store of Rama, the Maori name for the Torlesse Range as well as a peak in the Southern Alps.

WHATAMONGO: Correctly Whatamango; *whata:* food store; *mango:* shark. Store house for shark flesh.

WHATAROA : *whata :* store house; *roa:* long. Long store house.

WHATATUTU : *whata:* store house; *tutu:* shrub. Store house near the tutu bushes.

WHATAWHATA: elevated food store.

WHATITIRI :   thunder. Ihenga chanted a *karakia* on the hill, and the thunder roared as the chant ended.

WHATORO: to stretch out, or to thrust forward.

WHAU : a native tree. The Maori name for Avondale.

WHAWHAPO :   *whawha:* to feel about; *po:* night. A young chief crawled into a camp and felt about with his hands at night.

WHAWHARUA : *whawha:* to feel about; *rua:* pit. To feel about in the store pit.

WHEKENUI :   *wheke:* octopus; *nui:* big. Te Wheke-muturangi is the name of the huge octopus that 'Kupe chased across Cook Strait and finally killed in Whekenui Bay.

WHENUAHOU :   *whenua:* land; *hou:* new. New country.

WHENUAKITE : The full name, compressed by the Pakeha to Fenukit, is Te Whenua-i-kite-te-manu-aute-o-Tama-pahore, the land discovered by the paper-mulberry kite of Tama-pahore. This man flew a kite at Remuera. The string broke. The kite was followed until it came to earth at this place.

WHENUAKURA: *whenua:* land; *kura:* red. The name was brought from Hawaiki by Turi of the Aotea canoe, and given in memory of the red feathers of a tropic bird.

WHENUANUI: *whenua:* country; *nui:* big. Plenty of land.

WHENUAPAI: *whenua:* country; *pai:* good. Good land.

WHETUKURA: *whetu:* star; *kura:* red. Red star.

WHIRINAKI: to lean, or the buttress of a house.

WHITIANGA: the crossing, or the ford.

WINGATUI: Possibly the correct name is Whiringatua, the place of the plaiting of straps. There is a story that comes from the founding of Otago. It is said that one of the settlers shot at and winged a tui.

WIRI: Named after Takaanini Wirihana, a Maori chief. Wirihana is Maori for Wilson. Literally, To shiver, or tremble.

APPENDIX

EUROPEAN PLACE NAMES

THE following European names are mentioned in the text. The Maori names which follow may be the original names, or may contain a reference to the European place name in the text. Some suburbs having Maori names are also listed under the cities.

ALUM CREEK: Waimangeo
ANDERSON'S BAY: Puketai
ARROW RIVER: Haehaenui
      Kimiakau
ASHBURTON RIVER: Hakatere
ASPIRING, MOUNT: Tititea
ATHENS: Atene
AUCKLAND: Akarana
    Kahu
    Kohimarama
    Kohua-ora
    Mangere
    Manukau
    Manurewa
    Maungakiekie
    Mokoia
    Oka
    Onehunga
    Otahuhu
    Owairaka
    Papakura
    Papatoetoe
    Pupuke
    Rangitoto
    Remuera
    Takapuna
    Tamaki
    Tauranga-mango
    Taurarua
    Te Kurae-o-tura
    Te Papapa
    Te Ranga-o-Taikehu
    Te Tatua
    Te To

AUCKLAND: Titirangi
    Waiatarua
    Waikomiti
    Waitakere
    Waitemata
    Whau
AVON, RIVER: Orotore
    Otakaro
    Otautahi
AVONDALE: Whau

BALCLUTHA: Iwikatea
BAY OF ISLANDS: Kahuwera
    Kerikeri
    Kororareka
    Motu-arohia
    Moturoa
    Paihia
    Peowhairangi
    Taiamai
    Tokerau
BAY VIEW: Petane
BEN OHOU: Aroaro-kaihe
BEREA: Peria
BETHANY: Petane
BETHLEHEM: Peterehema
BISHOP'S PENINSULA: Huri-o-te-wai
BLENHEIM: Waiharakeke
BLIGH SOUND: Te Anahawea
BLUE LAKE: Tikitapu
BLUFF: Motupiu
BOULDER BANK: Te Pokohiwi
BOWEN FALLS: Hine-te-awa
BREAKSEA SOUND: Huihui-koura

GREYMOUTH : Mawhera
GREY RIVER : Mawhera
    Moutapu
GREYTOWN : Houhou-pounamu
GROVE ARM : Iwirua

HAAST PASS : Tiori-patea
HALL'S ARM : Kahui-kakapo
HAMILTON : Kirikiriroa
HASTINGS : Heretaunga
HAWKE BAY : Te Matau-a-Maui
HEN AND CHICKEN ISLAND : Te
    Kupenga-a-Taramainuku
HOLDSWORTH, MOUNT : Taratahi
HOWICK : Owairoa
HUTT VALLEY : Epuni
    Heretaunga
    Moera
    Naenae
    Petone
    Pomare
    Taita
    Te Ahi-a-manono
    Waiwhetu

INVERCARGILL : Waikiwi

JACKSON'S HEAD : Kupenga-a-Kupe
    Te Tao-o-Kupe
JERUSALEM : Hiruharama
JUDEA : Te Huria
JUDGE'S BAY : Taurarua

KIDNAPPERS, CAPE : Tapuwaeroa
KING COUNTRY : Rohepotae

LAODICEA : Raorikia
LAWYER'S HEAD : Te Ika-a-Parehika
LEVIN : Horowhenua
LINTON : Te Kairanga
LITTLE BARRIER ISLAND : Hauturu
LONDON : Ranana
LYALL BAY : Maranui
LYTTELTON : Okete-upoko
    Te Whakaraupo

MCKENZIE COUNTRY : Aorangi
MCLAREN'S PEAK : Matapehi-o-te-
    rangi
MACEDONIA : Makeronia
MARTON : Tutaenui
MAYOR ISLAND : Tuhua
MERCURY HARBOUR : Whanganui-o-
    Hei

MILFORD SOUND : Piopiotahi
    Te Pari
MOONLIGHT GULLY : Ko-kohaka-
    ruruwhenua

NAPIER : Ahuriri
    Hukarere
    Keteketerau
    Marewa
    Pania
    Upoko-poito
NELSON : Horoirangi
    Koputiraha
    Maitai
    Tahunanui
    Wakapuaka
    Wakatu
NEW PLYMOUTH : Ngamotu
    Paritutu
NILE RIVER : Waitakere
NORMANBY : Ketemarae
NORTH CAPE : Muriwhenua
NORTH ISLAND : Eaheinomauwe
    Nukuro
    Te Ika-a-Maui

ONE TREE HILL : Maungakiekie

PACIFIC OCEAN : Moana-nui-a-Kiwa
PALLISER, CAPE : Te Kawkawa
PALMERSTON NORTH : Awapuni
    Hokowhitu
    Papaioea
PANMURE : Mokoia
PASSAGE ISLAND : Motu-tawaki
PELORUS SOUND : Te Hoiere
PEPIN ISLAND : Huri-o-te-wai
PHIL.PPI : Piripai
PICTON : Waitohi
PORT CHALMERS : Koputai
PORT LEVY : Koukou-rarata
PORT NICHOLSON : Poneke
    Te Whanganui-
    a-Tara
PROSPECT, MOUNT : Haumaitikitiki
PROVIDENCE, CAPE : Kourariki
PUMPKIN FLAT : Te Papapa

QUAIL ISLAND : Otamahua
QUEEN CHARLOTTE SOUND :
    Arapaoa
    Motuora

RAINBOW MOUNTAIN : Maungakara-
    mea

RICCARTON: Putaringamotu
RIVERTON: Pukorokio
RUSSELL: Kororareka
Maiki

ST. JOHN, LAKE: Waiatarua
SAMARIA: Hamaria
SCINDE ISLAND: Hukarere
SEATOUN: Turanga
SEFTON, MOUNT: Aroaro-kaihe
SELWYN RIVER: Waikerkeri
SHAG POINT: Arai-te-uru
SHEERDOWN, MOUNT: Te Pari
SHELLY BEACH: Oka
Tauranga-mango
SHIP COVE: Meretoto
SILBERHORN, MOUNT: Aorangi
SINCLAIR HEAD: Rimurapa
SMYRNA: Hamurana
SOMES ISLAND: Matiu
SOUTHERN ALPS: Ka-puke-maeroero
SOUTH ISLAND: Arahura
Arapaoa
Kaikoura
Mahunui
Ta Wai Pounamu
Te Waka-a-Maui
SPEY RIVER: Kahui-kakapo
STEVENS ISLAND: Huihui-koura
STEWART ISLAND: Rakiura
Te Puka-a-Maui
STOP ISLAND: Motukiekie
SUMNER, LAKE: Hakakura

TASMAN, MOUNT: Horokoau
TEICHELMANN, MOUNT: Aorangi
THREE KINGS: Te Tatua
THREE KINGS ISLAND: Manawa-
tahi

TOM BOWLING BAY: Kapo-wairua
TORLESSE, MOUNT: Whataarama
VICTORIA, MOUNT: Hataitai
WARKWORTH: Mahurangi
Puhinui

WATCHMAN, THE: Te Kupenga-a-
Taramainuku
WEEKS ISLAND: Puketutu
WELLINGTON: Hataitai
Karori
Makara
Maranui
Matairangi
Muritai
Ngaio
Ngauranga
Ohariu
Ohiro
Otari
Rongotai
Te Aro
Te Kaminaru
Tinakori
Turanga
WELLINGTON HARBOUR:
Hataitai
Matiu
Poneke
Te Whanganui-a-Tara
WEST COAST: Poutini
Te Ika-a-Maui
WHALE ISLAND: Moturata
WHITE ISLAND: Whakaari
WILTON: Otari
YOUNG NICK'S HEAD: Te Kuri-a-
Pawa

ZION: Hiona